John Kluge Stories

John Kluge Stories

Introduction
John Kluge, Jr.

A Winterhouse Edition

Distributed by
Columbia University Press
2009

John Kluge Stories

PUBLISHER:
Winterhouse Editions
www. winterhouse.com/editions
DISTRIBUTOR:
Columbia University Press
www.cup.columbia.edu
DESIGN:
Winterhouse Studio
EDITOR:
Jan Werner
PRINTING:
Finlay Printing

© 2009 Winterhouse
P.O. Box 159, Falls Village, CT 06031

FIRST EDITION: SEPTEMBER 2009
ISBN 10: 1-884381-26-X
ISBN 13: 978-1-884381-26-3

For my father, who taught me that
sometimes the most important words
are never spoken.

With admiration and respect,
John

John W. Kluge and John W. Kluge, Jr., 1989, in the cabin at Morven Farm, Albermarle, Virginia. This historic farm was later donated to the University of Virginia.

Preface John Kluge, Jr.

This is not the book I intended to write. In fact, this book wasn't written as much as it was edited or maybe even collaged…. But let's back up a bit.

My father has led a very interesting life. Penniless boy arrives at Ellis Island, and through hard work, luck, and pluck, makes a tremendous success of himself: It's our favorite American story, and it's my father's story. That's one reason I wanted to write his biography. His story really is like a fairy tale come true.

I had a more personal reason too; I wanted to get to know my father. He was sixty-eight when I came into the picture, so there was very little rough-housing on the carpet or playing catch in the yard. At a time when most people's careers have slowed down or stopped altogether, he was still very much involved in the business of running his far-flung businesses. (In fact, I now realize that my early childhood coincided with the riskiest, most stressful time of his career.) Then, after my parents divorced, I experienced the loss any child feels when one parent—however loved and loving—just isn't there as much.

My father is an enthusiastic Columbia alumnus and while I was at his alma mater, we started becoming closer. He told me lots of stories about his time there, which made me want to hear more stories, about more episodes in his long and varied life. Thanks to my father, I have the luxury of working on projects that interest me—and this one did.

And so, after I graduated college, I moved in with my father for the summer. I had it all planned out. We'd spend our time discussing life and love and the complexities of existence.

We'd break bread together and share bad jokes. I'd get to know him and he'd get to know me. What I had in mind was a *Tuesdays with Morrie*-type of experience. What I got was... not that.

Trying to record our conversations made everything strained and awkward, and it started to feel like we were two strangers stuck in an elevator together for three months. So I banished the gadgets and resorted to the time-honored journalism practice of taking notes with pen and paper. I scribbled a lot of gibberish that summer, mostly on the back of gin scoring notebooks, because playing gin was just about all we did, all summer long. The three months I spent as my father's card pigeon will be my most treasured memory of him. We never had those lengthy conversations about dreams and poetry, but we did reach each other. We talked about lots of things, most of them inconsequential but invaluable. By the end of the summer, he told me he loved me, that he was proud of me—and that meant more than I can describe.

Okay, maybe *Mondays with Kluge* was not a book that would ever be written. What about a straightforward description of a long, eventful, and influential life?

That September, I started research for a more traditional biography of my father. I dug into the events of his life, starting with contemporaneous press accounts, old Metromedia files, and my father's randomly collected personal papers. I gathered information about events and topics that were important at various times in my father's life. I also interviewed his friends, other family members, former colleagues—even the young British boy, now grown, who survived brain cancer due to surgery paid for by my father. All that said, my chief source was my father himself. He's been interviewed many times, including three lengthy sessions for the Columbia Oral History Project, the Library of Congress, and most recently the National Parks Service, which is researching the history of Box 1142 where he served during WWII.

I discovered two obvious, universal facts: Writing a book is hard. Writing a book about one's parent is even harder. Yes, I know... anyone could have told me that. In fact, a few people did—but who was listening? Not me! There's a less universal fact that applies to anyone attempting to write about someone who's lived as long and done as much as my father—the scale of the project is pretty overwhelming. *Caveat scriptor.*

So the book I intended to write currently resides somewhere in the dungeons of my computer hard drive. Maybe one day I'll write the remaining chapters and complete my father's biography, but not until the story itself is complete.

What follows in the pages ahead are some of my father's stories, told by him. It is not his autobiography or a portrait of his family and children (yes, he has a few) or even a how-to guide for living a long and successful life. These are the stories he likes to tell, the ones that are most meaningful to him. I've collected them here as a way of honoring the man that I have grown to know and love so much.

If you're looking for a guidebook on gambling, poker, or gin, I suggest you look elsewhere, as he will never give up those secrets.

Index

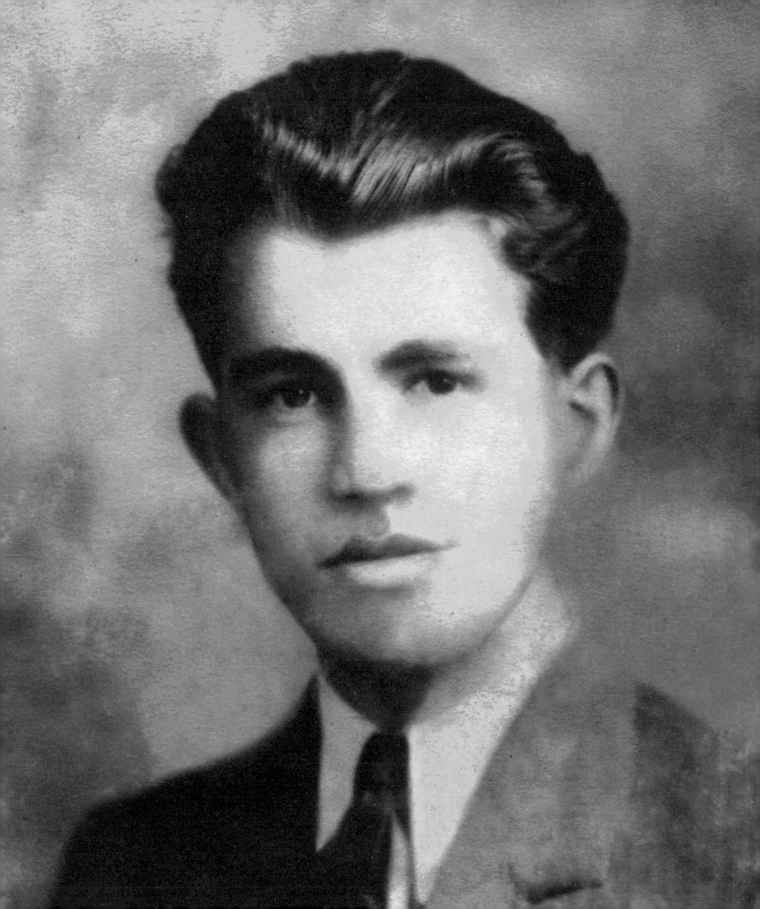

The world doesn't owe anybody anything, because it's all within yourself. I can't remember when I ever complained about my life. I always thought my life was wonderful. I really did, even when I didn't have a penny.

John Kluge On Life

I was born in Chemnitz, Germany.

Chemnitz was a manufacturing town. They made automobiles, and they made clothing such as gloves and other items.

I was born on September 21st, 1914. My father was killed in World War I, before I was born. He was an engineer, in metals. He and his family were Catholics, my mother and her family were Lutherans, and that didn't sit very well. You know, the same thing happened with my grandmother, my mother's mother. She came from Alsace-Lorraine and so she had a French background, and when she married a German — a lawyer — that was enough to send everyone ballistic.

My mother and my grandmother brought me up, and my mother never talked about my father. Isn't that funny? All I know is, his first name was Fritz. My mother never said much about her life at all. My uncle married but he never had children, and my aunts died early. One was a prima donna at the Dresden Opera House, and she committed suicide. I'm the only child of that whole family. They're all dead. I have no cousins. I was the only child my mother had. She said she couldn't handle two of us.

When I was five, a friend of my mother's promised me a toy locomotive for Christmas.

Well, the day came and she didn't arrive so I trudged for miles until I finally got to her house. The woman said she didn't have the locomotive. I cried — not in front of her, but all the way back home. And do you know, every time I see a locomotive I think of that. I remember it as if it happened today.

It's a funny thing. Some people promise you something just to make you feel good in the moment but maybe they have no intention of following through. That's a disappointment. That's why if I say I'm going to do something, I make very sure I do it. All my life, I've had a commitment to keeping my promises, and that's partly the underpinning of it.

KLUGE

Above: Views of Chemnitz early in the twentieth century.

Above: Chemnitz and surrounding area.

Opposite: John Kluge's stepfather, Oscar Leitert, was born in Germany but became an American citizen as a young man. Seen here picking oranges in St. Augustine, Florida.

Chemnitz, Germany
Stepfather

Top: The Kluge family in Scheinau. John Kluge (center) and Gertrude Kluge (right) with unidentified friends.

Bottom: An older John Kluge in Detroit.

Mother
Grandmother
Childhood
Grocery shopping
Favorite candy

Our diet was very simple: cabbage and potatoes, and once a week an egg.

My mother worked as a typist, six days a week, and my grandmother took care of me, and did the cleaning and cooking. Our diet was very simple: cabbage and potatoes, and once a week an egg. My grandmother would send me to the market with a shopping list and money, and I would bring back the groceries and the change. Well, prices were changing all the time and I realized I was the only one who knew how much the items cost. So if potatoes cost half a mark each, I said it was a little more than that, .55 marks, and gave her the change for that. I kept the difference. Every couple of weeks, I'd go to the candy store and buy, oh, whatever they had. Lollipops, gumdrops, sugar sticks. My favorites were Tootsie Rolls.

One day I said that a head of cabbage had cost more than an egg. My grandmother noticed that right way. *Nothing* was more expensive than eggs! I said I'd just mixed up the two numbers, and I was more careful the next week.

John Kluge and his mother, after the move to Detroit.

I always played for keeps.

Our building was situated next to a park, and I think that's why I always like a lot of grass and open space. In the summer we played games, hide-and-seek and so forth, and in the winter we had snowball fights. The boys also played marbles. I used some of my candy money and I bought a red agate marble, a shooter.

I've always been a gambler and in those years, I gambled for nebs, the little marbles. You could play a game where everyone went home with the same marbles they brought, or you could play for keeps, meaning that the wins counted. I always played for keeps. Every marble I knocked out of the circle, I kept. I kept a lot. I won over two thousand nebs from the other boys. Then they wouldn't play marbles with me anymore.

KLUGE

Mother
Grandmother
Childhood
Gambling
Scheinau, Germany

18

After the end of the war, things were still very hard in Germany.

Also, in this tenement house, there were always things broken, and I had a hand in some of that but I didn't break everything. I think the landlords were glad to see me go. Anyway, my mother and my grandmother decided it would be better to live somewhere out of the city and so we went to Scheinau to look at places to live. They found an apartment and they were negotiating with the landlord about the rent, and meanwhile I was looking around to see whether there were any children around. I didn't see any, so I made up my mind I didn't want to live there.

One day I went back out to Scheinau on, I remember, a maroon bus. Buses were new—at least they were new to me—and I loved riding that bus. I loved it so much I rode far beyond where I was supposed to get off and I had to walk back. I saw the landlord and I said to him, "My mother and my grandmother have changed their mind."

He asked me, "What about the deposit?"

I said, "Keep it."

Twenty-eight days later we drove out to Scheinau in a horse and wagon, and the few belongings we had in a trunk. As we were getting closer and closer to the house, I started to sweat. I knew there'd be an explosion. We saw the landlord and I hid between my mother and my grandmother, behind their skirts. The landlord said, "You cancelled the lease."

"We didn't cancel," my mother said.

And he said, "There's a little boy that came out and canceled, and there he is."

Oh, I trembled between these two ladies! We had to go back to the tenement house, which I was very glad to do, but my uncle gave me a real whipping. I must tell you, I remember that whipping like it was yesterday.

We did move to Scheinau, to the same building. The landlord found us another space, and I finally was resigned to the new quarters.

He'd bring us both to the United States.

My mother met Oscar Leitert in Scheinau. He was born in Germany but he'd lived in the U.S. since he was thirteen and he'd become an American citizen. He was in Scheinau visiting friends, and these were friends of my mother too. He told my mother he wanted to marry her. He had to go back to the United States to manage his affairs but he would come back in two months to marry her, and then he'd bring us both to the United States. And that's what he did.

John Kluge, Oscar Leitert, Gertrude Kluge Leitert.

We left Scheinau in 1922.

We took a horse and cart to the train station in Chemnitz, and then took the train to Bremen. That took four days. The train tracks went right to the dock so we got off the train and right on to the ship, the USS *George Washington*. I remember the dining room. I got there the minute mealtime started and I left when it ended. In between, I ate. Every day, there was meat, potatoes, milk, soup, sometimes even dessert. I thought I'd died and gone to heaven.

Then I got seasick. That put an end to that.

Childhood
Scheinau, Germany
Chemnitz, Germany
Bremen, Germany
USS *George Washington*
Publicity

KLUGE

20

The lumberyard in Scheinau owned by John Kluge's uncle.

I went back to Chemnitz in 1996.

I said to the mayor, "Do me a favor—don't give me any publicity. After I leave the city, you can do all you want but I don't want any publicity while I'm there." He found that strange. I didn't find it strange at all. Just because I came from that town, that doesn't make me important. And I just don't want that kind of publicity. I don't like any publicity, to tell you the truth. If I've done a good job, I'll know it and I'll be happy with that. I don't need the publicity or the recognition. I like to see results, but without a lot of fanfare.

We didn't bring much with us when we left Germany.

I had to leave my marbles, so I asked my grandmother to keep them for me. Later she and my uncle came to Detroit to live and I asked her where my marbles were. You know, she said she threw them out right after we left.

My mother packed a sailor suit, my best outfit, and she put me in charge of a Dresden figurine, a horseman, about a foot high. I remember we reached New York on September 15, 1922. My mother dressed me in that sailor suit and she gave me the statue to hold. I still have it. And every time I think I'm too smart for my own britches, I look at that horse and I know exactly where I came from.

The Dresden figurine
John Kluge carried
to the US

It really was a symbol of freedom.

When we got up on the deck, all the people were lined up, looking at the Statue of Liberty, crying and waving. It really was a symbol of freedom, and ever since I've had a soft spot for it. I have a maquette for another version of the statue, and it was refused on the basis that it was too fragile and the wind would damage it. That model is much more beautiful than the one that was eventually built. But of course I helped raise money to restore the statue for its centennial. You know, when the statue was first built, the head was brought to Madison Avenue and people gave their quarters and dimes and so on to help pay for the base of the statue.

Bartholdi maquette for an alternate Statue of Liberty design.

We arrived at Ellis Island.

We got through all the screenings and so forth, until the very end. My mother couldn't find my vaccination records and so I wouldn't be allowed in. One of the inspectors grabbed me to take me away and of course I didn't want to be separated from my mother, so I kicked him, as hard as I could. He didn't like that. He put me in a separate room and it was a very long time I was held, and I didn't like that. I didn't know what was going to happen to me. Finally they gave me the shots again and let me go.

Stature of Liberty, early 20th century.

KLUGE

The main hall of Ellis Island, c. 1920. After passing a brief inspection for obvious signs of disease, the immigrants were directed to separate "pens" to await further processing.

Children have a sense of awe and that's something we should never lose as adults.

The people who have the attitude of knowing everything are sad cases. A scholar knows that when he knows everything, he shuts his mind to anything new.

John Kluge On Know-It-Alls

We were in the very heart of New York.

We went first to the Taft Hotel, which was at Seventh Avenue and Broadway. One night my mother looked under the bed—I don't know why, it was just something women did then—and she saw a pile of German marks. She said, "What's this?" I had actually been filching them from my stepfather's pocket every night for a long time, just so I'd have money to go back if I didn't like it. They weren't worth much but I didn't know that.

Of course, by then I didn't want to go back. We were in the very heart of New York. I would stick my head out the window, see the fire engines, see everyone and everything in Times Square. For a boy of eight, it was very exciting.

Then we went on to Detroit, where my stepfather had his business. I was there about a month and I said to my mother, "I'm never going to live here."

KLUGE

Mother
Stepfather
Childhood
Taft Hotel
Times Square
New York, New York
Detroit, Michigan

28

"X" marks the spot. Times Square, c. 1920.

The Leitert house near Redford, Michigan, the second house John Kluge lived in after immigrating to America.

I didn't speak a word of English.

My stepfather had been married before and his first wife and their children lived in a big wooden house. He had a son and a daughter, both older than me. My mother and I stayed in something of a converted store, attached to the house. He was a painter and he had a shop built onto the property too.

I didn't speak a word of English. Each morning, I walked a few blocks to the neighborhood parochial school, an evangelical Lutheran school. They called me "Hans the Hun." That started when a teacher picked me to write the numbers on the blackboard. I wrote on the board the German numbers and one of them—"fünf"—had an umlaut above it. You can imagine how the other students laughed at me. You know, I didn't like it and I would come home very much roughed up.

After that, I carried a dictionary under my arm, an English-German Webster's Dictionary. I carried it to school, to church, back home, everywhere I went. I took it to bed with me to read. If I saw something while I was walking and I didn't know the English word for it, I'd stop and look it up. I carried that dictionary for ten years. I was determined to speak English, and without an accent.

And I wanted to be John Kluge. Nobody other than my family called me Johannes anymore.

We had been in Detroit about a year.

My stepfather sold the house in the city and bought a small farm near the town of Redford, and that's where we all lived.

The Europeans don't celebrate Thanksgiving, but in Redford we had some German neighbors who invited us over for Thanksgiving. The Papes were huge people. Very large. Mrs. Pape went into the kitchen and cut up the two turkeys. I remember so well, she gave me a plate with mashed potatoes and gravy, and the two turkey necks. She said, "Hans, how do you like the turkey?" I said, "I don't know. I don't have any." And my mother was mad. But two necks—you know, that's for the birds.

My uncle and I sold apples.

We had this little farm, and my uncle and I sold apples. My uncle and his wife and my grandmother all moved to Detroit in 1926 and lived near us in Redford. So we used to take the apples to market at three or four o'clock in the morning, but once in a while we would sell directly to homes. Once I said to my uncle, "Why don't you take one street, and I'll take the other." Then I ran like crazy ahead of him up his street to sell my apples. He'd come to a house and the people would say, "There's been a boy here already and we bought some apples from him."

Knowing that, when I saw my uncle, I told him, "You know, there must have been a little boy selling apples on my street, because I couldn't sell these people any."

I was a troublemaker, especially with my uncle. We had a plum tree and it was very small but I would be in the upper part, and I would wait with a rotten plum until my uncle walked under the tree. He was bald and I can see it yet, how that plum landed on his head and the juice ran down the side.

I didn't play any pranks with my stepfather because you didn't fool with him.

I always worked.

I swept the floor in my stepfather's paint shop. The fumes were bad, and rats and mice used to hide behind the paint containers. They weren't as big as the rats I saw later in the Aleutian Islands, during World War II. *They* were huge. And they would sit on their back legs and look right at you. I had bigger boots then so I wasn't as scared as when I was a boy.

Then I started cutting lawns. I learned very early that all you had was time, and there was only so much you could do in an hour. So to be an entrepreneur—which I seem to have been— I would employ these kids. Small lawns were twenty-five cents and I kept a nickel. Big lawns were fifty cents and I kept a dime. The biggest lawns were a dollar and I mowed those myself.

I had, oh, ten or twelve other boys working for me. I treated them like troops. I trained them: Always be polite to the customer. Don't talk to them unless they talk to you. And be neat. You can't do the job being a slob.

I would go to the homeowners in late winter, before anyone else was thinking about cutting grass. Once I had the work lined up, I found the boys to do it. But I always collected the money. And I made very sure those boys had no contact with the people, because otherwise I would lose my five or ten cents.

I also delivered newspapers, washed windows. I did a lot of odd jobs for people, especially older people. I turned most of the money over to my mother but I always kept a little bit of money on the side.

My stepfather didn't believe in education.

He wanted me to stop going to school after the eighth grade. That was all the education he thought necessary for a young man. He wanted me to go into the painting business with him. He already had his own children working for him, so I knew I would always be a second-class citizen. I would always be under his thumb. I convinced him to let me go on to high school, at least for one year. And so I skipped part of eighth grade and went straight to high school.

"What's the highest score you can make?"

At Northwestern High School, there were different houses, like home rooms, and you were assigned to one based on your last name and first initial. I was assigned to the Roosevelt House.

When I came in the first day, the man who ran the house was a real gentleman. His name was M.D. Jerome, and he would call every kid "Laddie." That way he didn't have to remember their names. Roosevelt House had a blackboard with the honor roll and the highest score there was a thirty-four. I said to Mr. Jerome, "What's the highest score you can make?"

"Forty."

"You're looking at forty."

I didn't have to do that, but the fact that I said to him what I did forced me to make forty, which I did. That's been my modus operandi. Even today, I live very much in a competitive mold, not because I want to but because that's my makeup and it has been for a long time.

I left home at fourteen.

After my first year of high school, my stepfather still wanted me to quit and join his business. I wanted to get more tools for bettering myself and he didn't believe in that, so I left home at fourteen.

There was no big scene. I still stayed in contact with my mother, and I never had any dislike for my stepfather. I was never really mad at him, because if it weren't for him, I wouldn't have come to this country and I would have been in Hitler's army.

Over the years, I don't know whether I was looking for a father, but I had a number of older men who were very generous with their time and advice. I listened to them, and they were good substitutes. Allen Crow was one. Teddy Prentiss was another. Elmer Auden, Judge Campbell. These were all men I respected and learned a lot from. But my stepfather, after I finished my first year in high school, said, "No more schooling." I either had to go into business, or I would have to leave home. I chose to leave home.

I was never afraid of making a decision.

It was an immediate decision, even though I didn't know where I was going to sleep the first night. I was never afraid of making a decision, regardless of the consequences. For a few days, I slept at the school and washed cars for food money. I waited until after dark so I could shower with the hose. Then I went to the home of one of my teachers, Gracia Gray DaRatt. She taught typing and shorthand in high school, and I took her classes and became quite proficient, which served me well. When I was at Columbia I was secretary to James Lin, the son of the president of China, and during the war I clerked for a general for a while.

I washed Mrs. DaRatt's car, and she asked me what I was doing. I said, "Well, I've left home," and I told her why and she took me in. She was a great woman but not someone to make a show. She said, "Here's the refrigerator, here's your bedroom, here's your bathroom," and that was it.

At fourteen, you're a boy. Between fourteen and eighteen, I became an adult. I grew up very fast. While there was never any pressure, I wanted to be what Mrs. DaRatt wanted me to be, and that was an outstanding student who would go to school beyond high school. She was a remarkable woman, and she encouraged me. She opened up my world. Remember, I was still rather constricted, in every way—in language, in religion, in education. She taught me manners, "the graces." She even introduced me to American foods, such as the baked potato. Corn. She was a very bright woman but quite pragmatic. Not a lot of warmth on the surface. If I had a cold she wouldn't say much, you know. She didn't pamper me at all, and that's good. She hoped that I would be an independent spirit, which she was. Tough American stock. She was all black and all white, nothing in between, and as you're growing up that might be a very good influence.

I listened to them and I learned.

I remember Mrs. DaRatt would have people over—doctors, businessmen, judges. I listened to them and I learned. Allan Campbell was a friend of hers. He was a judge, the founding dean of the Detroit City College Law School, and one night Judge Campbell was talking to a realtor about a piece of property he owned. You have to remember this was during the Depression, and the judge was going to lose some money on this property. And I remember this distinctly. The realtor said, "Well, you can do so and so and save some money." The judge said, "Oh, yes, I can do that legally—but not morally."

Things like that, these were sign posts to me. It's not how successful you are. Did you do it without being either a con artist or a person who was so burned up with success that anything goes? I don't feel comfortable with "anything goes." Never have, never will.

You know, the teacher said an interesting thing to me once. She said, "John, you're one of the few people I know who can learn from other people without going through the experience yourself." I felt that what they said—the judge, all these others—was so important, so meaningful, I could and should apply it to myself. It became important to do that.

Living with Mrs. DaRatt, little by little I formed a conclusion that I wanted to be somebody but not on the basis of cheating or fooling people. It's been a principle I've lived with; I've always been much more interested in substance than perception. If the substance is right, I feel that everything is right.

KLUGE

Adolescence
Gracia Gray DaRatt
Allan Campbell
The Great Depression
Success

36

John Kluge with Mrs. Gracia DaRatt.

"I'm more interested in substance."

There was a man who was on my board at one time until he said he had to get off, he's too busy. Well, then he went on another board, because that was more prestigious, and he felt that I wasn't his friend. He said, "You know, you don't like me anymore." I said, "No, no. I like you. But you and I are different. You are much more interested in perception. I'm more interested in substance. That's our difference." He wanted to not only be a CEO, he wanted to be perceived as a CEO.

I really don't care what people think as long as I think I'm doing the right thing. When I say I wanted to be somebody... remember, I was poor. I was uneducated. I had to go through all these steps. But being somebody had nothing to do with money. It was all about achieving something. There was a burning desire on my part to do something which made the world better.

What difference you can make, you should try to make.

In the sands of time, individuals make very little difference. But what little difference you can make, you should try to make. That's what I'm going to put on my tombstone, because there's too much avarice in the world, I think. There's too much competition for things that don't mean much in the long run. If you make a contribution that makes the world better, not only are you somebody, but you're implementing. I don't want to hurt anybody, and I don't want credit for it. I am not oriented toward getting credit. And so much of that came from the teacher.

In 1953, I was in St. Louis. I'd just closed a deal, buying a radio station in Clayton, Missouri, and I got the news of Mrs. DaRatt's death. I was the only person at her funeral. It was in the winter time, in Fairhaven, New York, and cold. I had to really take the gravediggers to task, because it was so cold they didn't want to get out of their hut. I remember so distinctly driving away, and I cried but the tears just froze, it was that cold. Bitter, bitter cold.

She was an inspiration for me. All my life I keep her memory.

Gracia Gray DaRatt
Epitaph
Implementation
St. Louis, Missouri
Clayton, Missouri
Fairhaven, New York
Amos and Andy
Katharine Cornell
Texas Guinan
Prohibition

While I was in high school I wrote for the student newspaper.

I interviewed people who were visiting Detroit, performers and writers, you know. I interviewed Amos and Andy. I remember, I said to Amos, "What did you do before you got into this business?"

He said, "I used to deliver meat packages to people."

"And what did Andy do?"

"He picked up the packages that I dropped on the way." They were funny in life, too.

I interviewed Katharine Cornell, who was a big Broadway actress. I didn't make too much headway with her. She had a suite at the Book-Cadillac Hotel in Detroit and it was dark and I stepped on one of her dachshunds. That was no way to get in Kathy Cornell's favor.

Texas Guinan, did you ever hear of her? Well, she was in a suite at the Book-Cadillac Hotel. I was interviewing her and I was embarrassed as hell because during the interview she was changing her dress. Answering the questions while she was undressing. She was in back of a screen but even so. I was quite young, of course.

Texas Guinan, c. 1930. In the silent film era, Guinan was "The Queen of the West," the first movie cowgirl. During Prohibition, she opened a speakeasy in midtown Manhattan and the 300 Club soon became a favorite hangout of actors, millionaires, and socialites.

In the sands of time, individuals make very little difference, no matter who they are, but what little difference you can make, you should try to make.

That's what I want on my tombstone.

John Kluge A Proposed Epitaph

I wanted to go to Columbia because it was in New York.

And not because it was Columbia. I knew I'd need a scholarship so I called Allen B. Crow, who was head of the Detroit Columbia Club.

[The following is Mr. Crow's recollection of the conversation, many years later.]

I received a phone call at home one evening. The caller asked, "Is this the president of the Columbia Alumni Club?"

I said, "Yes, it is."

"Do you have a scholarship available?"

"Yes, we do."

"Well, I want it."

"Do you have any money at all?"

"No, but I'll earn the rest. I'm willing to work my way through. But I want your scholarship."

Well, I admired the boy's pluck.

Low Memorial Library at Columbia University.

Columbia University
Allen Crow
Detroit Columbia Club
Scholarship
Ed Litchfield

KLUGE

42

"These hands will pull me through."

I applied for the scholarship and it came down to two fellows: Ed Litchfield and me. Ed was on the debating team, and he was very well-versed in the English language, while I really was not. I wore rough clothes and he was very refined. We both went to Mr. Crow's house for the interview and I said to Mr. Crow, "I'd like to be interviewed second, if you don't mind." So Ed was interviewed first. When Mr. Crow got to me, he asked various questions, the usual things. We were in his sun parlor. Then, as I'm walking to the front door, I turned and walked back. I said, "Mr. Crow, I don't know whether I'll get this scholarship, but I want you to look at my hands." They were very rough because I did a lot of work with my hands. I said, "I don't know whether I'm going to get this scholarship but even if I don't, these hands will pull me through." Well, I think that took Mr. Crow so by surprise.

I still think Litchfield should have gotten the scholarship. But he didn't get it. I did. Litchfield went to the University of Michigan. You know, he became president of Carnegie Tech at a later time. He was an outstanding fellow, certainly better material than I was.

I had very little chance to get the scholarship but I did.

The point is, I always felt that I could work my way through, and I did. I didn't feel the world owed me anything. As a matter of fact, I consider that, even today, a weakness. The world doesn't owe anybody anything, because it's all within yourself. I can't remember where I ever complained about my life. I always thought my life was wonderful. I really did, even when I didn't have a penny.

But I can't understand, even today, why anybody in this country who has his health can complain, because there are always opportunities. If somebody wants to work in this country, they can find work. Oh, sure, it may be cleaning windows, maybe cleaning sewers — whatever — but you can find a job.

When I got the scholarship, I wrote back and said it wasn't enough.

I was realistic enough to know that I needed an increase for me to go to New York. If they wanted me, they would do that; if they didn't want me, they'd say no and I would have to live with it. Mrs. DaRatt said, "You know, they're just going to tell you it's been nice to have made your acquaintance, but you go somewhere else because you're too rich for our blood." But that's the chance I took.

Well, they gave it to me, but it took a month or so to find out. That schoolteacher, she and I would stop at the post office every day—Box 63 at the Ferndale Post Office—and I would look into that little window for a white envelope with blue printing, and one day there it was. I came out to the car, a little Ford, and I showed the letter to Mrs. DaRatt. She said, "I'll bet they turned you down." I said, "I'll bet they didn't." And they didn't. They gave me the double scholarship.

I learn every day, even now.

Going to school is predominantly to discipline your mind. It's also to encourage you to go on learning throughout your life. I learn every day, even now. Children have a sense of awe and that's something we should never lose as adults. The people who have the attitude of knowing everything are sad cases. A scholar knows that when he knows everything, he shuts his mind to anything new.

I think a person needs curiosity, and a sense of enthusiasm. It doesn't matter what you're enthusiastic about. To be enthusiastic is to be a participant. It's a sign you're alive.

Gracia Gray DaRatt
Columbia University
Scholarship
Risk
Education
Grades

KLUGE

I remember getting ready for Columbia.

Mrs. DaRatt said, "You've got to have a tuxedo, and even tails," and she found some for me. I was standing at the tailor's as they were downsizing the tuxedo and the tails when I heard one of them say, "Isn't it too bad that so-and-so died?" So I knew these clothes had belonged to someone who was dead. I could never wear them.

My first roommate was Henry Galbraith, from El Paso, Texas. I kept telling him, "Henry, you go to dances and all this, you really ought to have a tuxedo and tails." I finally sold him the whole outfit for twenty dollars: five dollars down, five dollars a month. I didn't need a tuxedo after all. Beautiful material in it, though. The lining was pink.

I came to Columbia with fifteen dollars, and I left with seven thousand.

To get my scholarship, I had to really work — get all A's and that sort of stuff. When I went to college I didn't care. I didn't care about the Phi Beta Kappa or any of those things, because I had three or four jobs while I was in school and a lot of times I wouldn't sit down to my studies until midnight. I came to Columbia with fifteen dollars, and I left with seven thousand. I guess I got a B-average. That didn't bother me. I got what I wanted, and it wouldn't make any difference what my grades were, as long as they were passing.

I was always selling something.

At graduation they had a cemetery full of headstones for everyone in the class, with quotations on the stones. On my stone they put, "I'm wiser. I sold my body for fertilizer." I was always selling something.

I was a pricer at the John Jay Dining Hall, so I got my three meals. I had a stationery business. Every freshman who comes in wants to write to his friends, or his girlfriend, or his family, on the stationery of Columbia, with his name or his initials and the year he graduates. Being a pricer at the dining hall, I was able to say to students, "Is this your first year?" Yes. "Have you got any stationery?" He might say no. I'd say, "Give me your room number. I'll be up to see you." So being a pricer also gave me a place to sell stationery.

I gave personal service. I brought the stationery to them when it was finished. I did that, also, to collect the money. The printer wanted to get paid right away, so I had to collect the money right away.

In 1938, the *Detroit Times* had a contest, and I won second prize—$2,000. That was a lot of money then! I used part of it to buy Mrs. DaRatt a car.

I also cleaned motor rooms in boats on the river. I would work cleaning engine rooms on Saturday and I'd have grease all over me. It took half a day to get rid of the grease. I didn't want to come up to Columbia campus with all that grease.

I represented a shoe company, and I would go around the campus with one shoe under my arm. A guy said, "That's a good-looking shoe," and I'd say, "Come on up to my room. I've got the other one there." I represented a clothing store on 114th Street, and I got my clothes at a very deep discount.

Nothing really bothered me, because I needed the money to exist. Being a pricer, I got my meals. With the scholarship, I got my room and tuition and books. Any clothing I needed, any other money I needed, I got from the stationery or the odd jobs. And all the ways I raised my money were honest ways.

Gracia Gray DaRatt
Columbia University
Henry Galbraith
Epitaph
Stationery
Odd jobs
Detroit Times

Right: Clipping from the *Detroit Times*.
Following spread: Gracia DaRatt with what may be the car John Kluge bought for her with his contest winnings.

'It's Glorious,' Winner Of Second Prize Says

Excerpt from *Detroit Evening Times*, April 29, 1938

He's Giving a Car to Woman Who Tutored Him

BIG BOY JOHN W. KLUGE   MRS. GRACIA DA RATT
Mr. Kluge, 23, protege of Mrs. Da Ratt, Northwestern High School teacher, telling their dog Big Boy all about his good fortune. John won second prize of $2,000, will use some of it to buy his "foster mother" a new car, pay off his college debts, and lay the rest aside. He earns $30 a week.

Two thousand dollars for John W. Kluge—and as a corollary of his good fortune a new automobile for Mrs. Gracia DaRatt, a Northwestern High School teacher, whose protege Kluge has been since he was 16. These are the returns for perseverance and faith.

The $2,000 is awarded to 23-year-old Kluge as second prize in the $15,000 Famous Names Contest of The Detroit Times, winners of which are announced today. On Page 1 is a story on Gerald P. Herlihy, 100 Seward avenue, winner of the first prize of $10,000. The following concerns the three other major winners and elsewhere in the paper is a complete list of the 100 winners.

Kluge lives at the DaRatt home at 1974 Ariel road, Southfield Township. He is employed by Otten Brothers, makers of die cut cards, 7358 Richmond avenue.

TOOK HIM INTO HOME

"I owe a lot to Mrs. DaRatt," commented Kluge. "She took me into her home when I was 16 and virtually destitute. She helped me to obtain an education; she has encouraged me in my business—and she was an inspiration for me to do my best in the contest.

"Oh, it certainly is a grand and glorious feeling to win the $2,000! It means that I shall be able to pay off some debts contracted in obtaining my education at Columbia University, from which I graduated last year, put aside some money, and at the same time do something in a small way to help pay the vast debt of gratitude I owe Mrs. DaRatt. One of the first things I'll do with my windfall is to buy a new automobile for her.

"Work hard in the contest? I should say I did, but it is worth the while. Of course, I consulted lots of books for information, but I was able to draw a lot of the answers from the factual fund I got at Columbia. I feel just like a millionaire."

I am open to anything that improves the human condition.

I was never a card-carrying Communist. But I believed in the idea that everyone should contribute. Norman Thomas influenced me greatly. I heard him the first time when I was in high school; I was mesmerized by him. But, you see, the Communists started burning books and all kinds of things at Columbia, and that's when I left that idea.

I've never liked the establishment because I'm not interested in the status quo. As a matter of fact, change is what I really like. I'm not attached to things. I have things and I like them but if I lost them, I would still feel happy inside myself. In that respect, I'm a revolutionary.

In today's politics, I'm neither a Republican nor a Democrat. I am open to anything that improves the human condition. I'm fiscally conservative because someone has to pay for it. In that way I'm a conservative, but not many others.

Norman Thomas (center) in Manhattan's Union Square, on May Day 1931. Thomas was the leader of the Socialist Party in America during its heyday, the 1920s and '30s.

Columbia University
Politics
Communism
Norman Thomas
Gracia Gray DaRatt
James Lin
New York, New York

KLUGE

50

I learned a lot from Jim Lin.

Grace DaRatt said, "John, you're going to go far, because you listen." Actually, I listen a great deal more than I talk. I was secretary to the son of the President of China, and I studied the Mandarin language for six months. James Lin was son of Lin Sen, the president after Sun Yat-Sen and Chiang Kai-Shek.

I learned a lot from Jim Lin. One day we were taking the subway, and you know in New York it's a rush for the subway. He said, "How often do these subways come?" I said, "Every three minutes." He said, "So we'll wait three minutes." He taught me a lot about patience. And, you know, it paid off later. We had a cellular operation in Shanghai, the largest city in China—thirty million people then. The Chinese government said, "Look, we don't want you to own our system. We don't want outsiders to own any part of our telecommunications." I agreed heartily. I said, "I understand your policy." They paid us back ninety million plus interest. Some companies want to fight it. My feeling is, you never fight the Chinese. They have the patience of Job, and they would tie you up so you would never get what you wanted. It's better to give in to their request, and so you learn.

Jimmy Lin was one of my best customers for the stationery business, and I invited him to come to Detroit with me over the winter break in 1933.

When we pulled into Michigan Central in Detroit, the shades in the sleeping car were all down. I put up the shade, and I saw all of these people out on the platform. And, I said to Lin, "There's got to be somebody important on this train." Little did I think it was for Lin, you know.

Jim had an eye with the ladies.

Everything with him was percentage. We'd walk on the street, he'd say, "That girl is eighty-five percent. That one is fifty percent."

And he had a pretty good grasp of American slang. While we were in Detroit, he needed a haircut so I took him to a barber shop. This barber had Jim turned around, facing away from the mirror, while he was cutting Jim's hair. When he was done, Jim looked in the mirror and saw the guy had cut it too short. Jim was kind of a small guy and this was a great big barber. Jim looked at him and he said, "You son of a bitch."

The year after we went to Detroit, the Chrysler Company offered me a job as their representative in China. They said they'd pay me $10,000 in salary and at that time, ten thousand dollars a year was a lot of money. I was tempted. I asked Ted Prentiss what I should do. He said, "Look, you finish your education. If they want you at the end of your graduation, you can always go with them then." Well, that was very good advice, though of course I didn't go with them after all.

Right: James Lin, John Kluge, and three of the Detroit civic leaders who organized their tour of the city. (Lin, center front; Kluge, back, to the right of Lin.

Opposite: Lin, Allen Crow, Kluge. Crow was the head of Detroit's Columbia University Club, which awarded Kluge a scholarship and then doubled it. Crow remained Kluge's lifelong friend and supporter.

Detroit, Michigan
James Lin
Chrysler Company
Allen Crow
Teddy Prentiss
Gracia Gray DaRatt

KLUGE

52

John Kluge and
James Lin, in Mrs.
DaRatt's house.

Detroit Heaps Honors on Columbia Students

Ford, Chrysler Fete Son of China's President

Excerpts from *Detroit Times*, January 1934

Jim Lin and John Kluge Receive Keys to City, View Art, Relics, Society. Rival Magnates to Entertain Pair on Holiday Visit

".... Were Jim and I surprised!" said Kluge last night, speaking of the rousing welcome. "For awhile there I was kind of worrying about entertaining Jim right..."

...Then the short-trousered dining hall cashier told how he and Lin became close friends.

"I first met Jim while making the rounds of the dormitories trying to sell stationery. He nearly bought me out the first night I saw him.... Four weeks before the Christmas vacation began I asked him to come to Detroit with me. Jim is doing graduate work in economics, and I thought he'd be interested in taking a look at the automobile plants... On the train," continued Kluge, "I was worried, trying to figure out just how Jim was going to like being mauled [sic] around in a Detroit street car. An executive from Chrysler Motors solved that problem by telling us that the private car of Walter P. Chrysler would be at our disposal through the holidays. There are only eighty cars in the world like Mr. Chrysler's, and the queen of England has one.

"While we were dining at the home of my guardian, Mrs. Gracia DaRatt, Mr. Crow read out our schedule for the holidays. I had no appetite that day. How could a fellow eat after being told he was to meet Henry Ford at dinner?"

On the list of social engagements were visits to the Chrysler, Ford, Dodge, and Packard plants, which Lin insisted on inspecting carefully. The bland Chinese was interested in the mass production methods employed.

"That's what we're going to have in China," he told an interviewer.... [Kluge fainted during a tour of Parke-Davis Drug company.] "They took me to the infirmary," he said. "And they let me have the prettiest nurse I've ever seen. When Jim saw her, he wanted to swat himself on the head and get in the bed right beside me, but the directors wanted him for lunch."

Automotive assembly line, c. 1933.

We agreed to meet in Baghdad.

Another of the fellows I met at Columbia was Baba Ali, who was a son of Sheikh Mahmud Barzanji, the exiled king of Kurdistan. We agreed to meet in Baghdad at noon, August 14th, 1936. That summer I visited Cairo. I went to Israel, which was Palestine then. There were camels on the streets in Tel Aviv. I traveled all around the region but on August 14th, there I was in Baghdad, on Rashid Street, which is the main drag. Then it was just a dirt road, like a frontier town in a Western. I'd said I'd be there and I was—but he wasn't!

Well, Baba Ali did show up finally, with his driver, and we drove across the desert in his Cadillac, up to his family's home. I lived a month up in the hills, in Kurdistan. They treated me very well, though I remember one night we visited a Moslem holy man, removing our shoes at the door, of course. He brought me grapes. "Here, infidel, eat," he said. "You are a welcome guest in my house."

It was a different culture. For example, Baba Ali had great eyes and he could hunt like crazy. But we went fishing one day and he threw dynamite in the water and all these fish just came floating to the top. That's how he went fishing.

I said to him one day, "Baba Ali, I saw this beautiful girl in the courtyard." He said, very serious, "Let me tell you, that's my sister and you never saw her. Don't ever speak about it, because if you do somebody will kill you."

You know, it was quite an experience.

Sheikh Mahmud Barzanji. In 1919, Barzanji led the first Kurdish rebellion against British rule and continued the opposition even while in exile. Eventually the British were forced to recognize Kurdish autonomy; Barzanji reigned as the first King of Kurdistan from 1922 to 1924, when the British once again took control.

KLUGE

I was a gambler.

I gambled with sugar heirs from Cuba, anyone who wanted to play. One day the dean of Columbia College asked me to come to his office. He said, "You know, we don't understand you. You're gambling all night and you're here on that scholarship." I said, "Dean, you'll never catch me gambling again." That's the first time I realized the dean of Columbia College didn't understand the English language. I didn't say I wouldn't gamble again, I said he'd never catch me again.

I remember playing stud poker and five card, with the first card down and the next four up. One night I had a five up and the next card was a five. The two after that didn't mean much but the third card was a five—three fives. Just as the betting was really getting hot, there was a knock on the door. We had all agreed that as soon as there's a knock, all of the cards will go under the table and be cancelled out. So the cards went away and I opened up a book. The door opened and believe it or not, it was a guy who had a headache and wanted some aspirin. I never knew that a headache could be transferred that quickly. So ever since, there have been three fives always landing in my mind.

When I bought the DuMont television stations, they had a Channel 5 in New York and they had a Channel 5 in Washington. I went up to Boston to buy their Channel 5, and I borrowed the money, two hundred and twenty-two million. I said, "You've got a week to decide," because I didn't want them to shop the station and run up the price. And that's how I got the three fives together for Metromedia.

They took my appendix out for no reason.

My roommate introduced me to beer. I was pretty woozy from that first drink. We came back to the dormitory and I went to the lavatory—there was just one common one on each floor. Well, I looked in the bowl and there was blood. I ran down to our rooms and I said to my roommate, "I'm dying!"

We went directly to St. Luke's Hospital and they took my appendix out. I was there ten days and when I came back, we had a powwow on the floor. This one fellow asked me, "Why did you go to the hospital?"

I said, "I was bleeding, the night of so-and-so."

He took me down to the lavatory and he said, "Which stall?" I showed him. He said, "That's the night I had a nosebleed." They took my appendix out for no reason. But while I was there, I met a very nice young woman, a nurse there, and we went out for some time. So something good came out of it.

"Outstanding people want to be with outstanding people."

Columbia, I think, is a great institution. Nicholas Murray Butler was president of the university while I was there—both before and after, until the 1940s. One time, I asked him, "Dr. Butler, how is it you're able to keep some of these professors here?" He said, "I'm going to tell you. Outstanding people want to be with outstanding people. They don't want to be alone. It doesn't stimulate them." I think he's right, and Columbia's had some great people.

Nicholas Murray Butler. Butler was president of Columbia University from 1902 to 1945. During his long tenure, he reshaped the campus and the university itself. A prodigious fundraiser, he used the contributions to add new schools and departments, as well as the new buildings to accommodate them.

When you have nothing, why not take a risk?

There was a professor, Armin K. Lobeck, and he was in geology. He mesmerized me, my second year at Columbia. He made geology so interesting, I thought I would become a geologist—specifically, a paleontologist—and would probably work for an oil company, traveling the world. But in my third year and then, reinforced by my fourth year, I thought it over and I decided I wanted to go into business. I think basically I always wanted to go into business, but this geology course was so interesting, Professor Lobeck made it so interesting, that I darned near changed my mind. If I'd gone in that direction, I can tell you one thing—I would have been a wildcatter. My instincts are always to take a risk. I like taking risks. I guess it's like an addiction. My addiction is taking a risk. When you have nothing, why not take a risk? You can only fall on your face.

I know this sounds crazy, but I don't really like a sure thing. It doesn't give me any excitement. As I got older, the risks became more calculating. I felt they would be worthwhile, they would succeed, and it often turned out that way.

And though I like risks, I don't go into them unprepared. I think about them a lot, and I try to read as much as I can. I'm an information junkie, a news junkie. I paid nine dollars once for a *New York Times* in Iran. I gather information and I consult with my people but then I have to make that decision.

Most often, I make it on the basis of—will we add something to this business? I am oriented to improving a product or service. Just me-too business, that's not interesting to me. Every business I've ever been in, my thoughts were always to improve what they're doing. It might not be successful, but I love taking a risk. I really don't like a sure thing. That doesn't give me any thrills.

Always be polite to the customer. Don't talk to them unless they talk to you. And be neat. You can't do the job being a slob.

John Kluge Advice to Boys Mowing Lawns

Jobs were still hard to get.

I never stayed for the graduation at Columbia. I worked that night, in Holyoke, Massachusetts. I graduated in 1937, and jobs were still hard to get. I went back to Detroit and I lived with Mrs. DaRatt to save money. I got a job as a shipping clerk at a small printing company, Otten Brothers. I've always felt you should start low. Before you ever become a boss, you'd better know the steps along the way. The worst thing in the world, from my point of view, is to start from the top. You have no feeling about the people under you, about the business.

After couple of weeks, I told them I'd work for no salary or commissions, only expenses, until I doubled the company's sales. I did it in eighteen months, and they made me a vice president. From shipping clerk to vice president in less than two years... well, you can imagine how big the company was. But I did double the sales. They went from $15,000 a year to $50,000. More than doubled—more than tripled.

I wanted to hear from the customer.

I went to Dallas, Texas, when I was working for Otten Brothers. The man I was visiting, he never asked me to sit down. He said, "You have rotten products, you have rotten service, you're a one-horse outfit." I was just standing there. I said to him, "Well, don't you feel sorry for me, working for a company like that?"

But I handled all his complaints, and I made it a special point to do that. I became very close to this man because he knew I was trying to rectify what he felt was definitely a lack on the part of this small company. The company had a reputation of, "Well, we'll ship your order," and they didn't want to hear from the customer. Well, I wanted to hear from the customer. It was a company of ethics, but lousy execution.

Gracia Gray DaRatt
Columbia University
Otten Brothers
Holyoke, Massachusetts
Detroit, Michigan
Dallas, Texas
Frugality

The Otten brothers were so tight, they rubbed off the buffalo on the nickels.

A dime was too much to carry around. It had to be in the bank. Elmer Otten was the president of the company. He was looking at my expense report, and I had five cents down for snacks. He said, "What's the five cents for?"

I said, "A Hershey bar. In the afternoon I need the energy."

He said, "Do you realize that a Hershey bar is nothing but sugar? When you're in a cafeteria, they have a bowl of sugar cubes. You take four or five of those and put them in your pocket. It's the same as a Hershey bar and it costs no money. You've been on the road forty weeks. Five cents a day, six days a week, that's thirty cents a week. You've spent twelve dollars of the company's money you didn't have to spend."

Then, as I was going out the door, he called me back. "Twelve dollars and forty-eight cents, because interest is four percent." He was so disgusted with me. He said, "I want to tell you something. You're never going to amount into anything." And he was damned near right.

When I came into television, which was a freewheeling business, I carried some of these ideas with me. We, the top fifty executives, would watch the travel, the hotels, the telephone, entertainment, meals—all the expenses, we kept down. One day I called an employee of ours in Kansas City. I said, "Joe, you won the prize last month."

He said, "I did? For what?"

I said, "Joe, you had the highest telephone bill in the company. And the only reason I'm calling you is I don't want you to win the prize next month." You know, not only did his phone bills go down, but everybody else's did too.

To this day, if I go into a restaurant in New York, I don't take a hat and coat. I'd have to check them, and that's an expense.

I always live up to my commitments.

Or I certainly try. One day I had an appointment in Buffalo and there was a snowstorm, a blizzard. It shut down the city and to shut down Buffalo, you know it had to be something. There were no taxicabs so I walked all the way out to where I had this appointment. I got there and I went all through the warehouse. Nobody was there, except a man at a desk off in a corner. He said, "What are you doing here?"

I said, "I have an appointment with Mr. So-and-so."

"How did you get here?"

"I walked here."

He was the owner of the business. He gave me the biggest order I'd had up to then. That stayed with me.

Twenty-five years later, I needed my first big multi-million dollar loan. I got an appointment with one of the major bankers in New York. I was in Chicago and a snowstorm blew in, from Chicago all the way east—but I had to be in New York at 9:00 o'clock the next morning. I flew out of Chicago but we had to land in Cleveland. I got hold of a taxicab, and we drove all the way to Pittsburgh. I got on a train and stood from Pittsburgh to New York—a long way. And when I got to New York, I had to walk from Penn Station to midtown. I had an appointment at 9:00 o'clock and I said I was going to be there, and I was.

I got up there and it was just like Buffalo. Nobody else was there except one man, and he said, "What are you doing here?"

"I have an appointment with Mr. So-and-so."

"Well, he isn't here. How did you get here?"

And I told him—Chicago to Cleveland, and then the taxicab and a train and walking uptown, because I had a 9:00 o'clock appointment.

He said, "You know, we have a committee that decides on these loans and the rest of the committee isn't here." He took me to the elevator. Then he said, "You know, I head the committee. And I just want you to know, you got the loan."

That experience in Buffalo, the point carried on all those years later.

Commitments
New York, New York
Buffalo, New York
Chicago, Illinois
Cleveland, Ohio
Midwest
Bronx Card & Paper Company
Pittsburgh , Pennsylvania
Manufacturer's Hanover Bank
Customers

KLUGE

To me, a good idea not implemented is no idea at all.

I always listened to my customers. I found out that this man named Kravis, who was with one of our larger competitors, he was charging different prices to different customers. He'd give discounts to customers in the Midwest, near us, but he kept his prices high in New York, where he was based. So I went to all these customers of ours and said, "I'll meet that price from Kravis but you'll have to give me a copy of your bills so I can show my president what we need to meet." They gave me copies all around.

Now, Kravis's biggest account was Bronx Card & Paper Company. The owner said to me, "Young man, I would like to give you some business but I have a friend who takes care of me, and he's taken care of me for many years." I said, "Well, Mr. So-and-So, are you sure he's taking care of you? I'm going to show you these bills. Your friend is selling merchandise in Buffalo and Pittsburgh below the price you pay." Oh, his face turned red. He gave me a carload of orders. So I spoiled Kravis's game.

I always try to analyze something before I move. To me, a good idea not implemented is no idea at all. There are plenty of ideas around. I am much more interested in implementation, what will get results.

Many years later, I was at a formal dinner and the president of Manufacturer's Hanover Bank came up to me. I was one of his heavy borrowers. He brought over an elderly man and the man said, "I'll bet you don't remember me." It was Kravis. Of course I remembered him. Kravis said, "When you went into the army, I prayed for you." And I thought to myself, "Yeah, you prayed that I'd never come back."

David Rockefeller.

I couldn't lead men if I weren't one myself.

I enlisted in the army in February 1941. At that time, if you volunteered, you got out after a year. Well, I was in the army four and a half years. I enlisted as a private. I always felt you have to start at the bottom. I couldn't lead men if I weren't one myself.

I did go to Officer Candidate School. When I was leaving, the first sergeant called me in and said, "I don't know why you're going to OCS. You'd make a great first sergeant."

I said, "I would?"

"Yes," he said. "You're the laziest son-of-a-bitch in the company."

At OCS, they trained me in military intelligence, at Camp Ritchie in Maryland. I remember Camp Ritchie very well, because once during the night maneuvers I sat on a nest of snakes. And, of course, they were copperheads. Maryland was loaded with copperheads. The man who got the most respect of all the people out there was from West Virginia. He'd pick up the copperhead and swing it around. Just snap its head off. I tell you, I thought he walked on clouds.

That's where I first met David Rockefeller though we didn't see each other again for years. We were not of the same social status at the time.

US Army
Officer Candidate School
Camp Ritchie
David Rockefeller
New York, New York
Chicago, Illinois
Chicago Tribune

I applied my military intelligence knowledge to my own business later on.

There was a mole in my company, and you can't deal with a mole directly. You can't let him know that you suspect him, and that's very important.

Now, Channel 5 in New York was a competitor of Channel 11, and Channel 11 was owned by the *Chicago Tribune*. I said to a whole group of people, while the mole was there, that we were going to bid for a syndicated show. I said, "We'll mortgage the whole company for this show. I don't think anybody knows it but we've done a lot of research that says if you own that show, you'll automatically bring the station up in ratings." Well, the mole passed that on to Chicago, and they bid and they bid and they bid. We didn't bid, so they got it. There were two shows coming up for syndication following this, which were good shows, and I could just see how Chicago would say to the management, "Let me tell you, you said this show would make the station. You paid a lot of money for this one, so forget about these other shows." Well, we bought these other shows and did very well with them.

If you suspect you have a mole and you want to identify him, it takes a lot of work. You pass out different pieces of information and then you wait for that information to come back and, depending on which piece it is, you know who the mole is.

I learned all that at Camp Ritchie.

Camp Ritchie.

She made up her mind I was a German spy.

They trained me in military intelligence but then they sent me out to March Field in California, in charge of a black engineer aviation unit. And then they sent me to the Aleutian Islands. I didn't find out for many years why that was. Not long before I enlisted, I took a young lady out to dinner. She was the niece of a woman who knew Mrs. DaRatt. I'd just come back from traveling in Europe, including Germany, and I told this young lady about the trip and about my plans to enlist. Well, she made up her mind I was a German spy. She wrote the Pentagon and they decided they were going to make sure I couldn't do any damage. They made sure I was cocooned.

I played my tricks on them.

When I was at March Field with this black unit, I played my tricks on them. We'd be marching on the base and when a pretty girl walked down the street, I would give them "eyes left," and as soon as she walked past I would give them "eyes right." But I fought for them in Riverside, in the town. After basic training, we'd go off the base and they'd buy a bottle of wine and sit in the park and drink the wine. And they would get in trouble for that. They were not hurting anybody, they were not bothering anybody, so I would absolutely stand up for them. I fought for them. I didn't care whether they're black, green or white, because they're human beings. It's amazing, what minorities faced. Years later, I refused to buy a radio station in Savannah, Georgia, because they were so anti-black. Maybe it's those first years in Europe, but I don't understand racism.

KLUGE

US Army
March Field
Aleutian Islands
Gracia Gray DaRatt
Racism
Savannah, Georgia
Marlene Dietrich

Marlene Dietrich came to March Field.

I got to introduce her to the troops. Boy, I tell you. She was then about fifty years of age, and she sure didn't look it. I didn't give her a long introduction. The minute she appeared, I said, "Here's Marlene Dietrich"—that's all that I could say, there was so much applause. I think she identified with them, and they felt that. She had a lot of empathy. And when she spoke, you'd get a tingle up and down your spine.

Marlene Dietrich, in the field with a US Army division.

The snow went sideways, sometimes straight up.

I have very vivid memories of Dutch Harbor. The rats were as big as rabbits. Not only did they sit on their hind legs, but they would glare at you. They weren't afraid of you. And there were so many of them around the kitchens and so on. We had these big boots on, so we didn't care. We would just walk around them, walk over them, whatever.

The weather might be very clear one minute and all at once, the clouds would come in and it's dark and cloudy for days and days. And the williwaws—the snow wouldn't fall down. It went sideways, sometimes straight up. That wind just keeps driving. You have to get used to it somehow.

A number of soldiers couldn't do that, and they committed suicide. They couldn't take it. They weren't balanced, and they couldn't take it. And that's understandable.

Most of what we had were fishing boats turned over to the military for the war effort.

But there were some nice ones too. The Zellerbachs, in San Francisco, had given up their yacht and we had it. My boss, the quartermaster, took it one afternoon for a private fishing trip. Well, we had all these ships arriving with 15,000 troops, and the ships couldn't dock at Dutch Harbor, so we had to ferry the men back and forth. I was frantic. I needed this boat. And I told the operator to cut everybody off. The quartermaster called me. He said, "Did you cut me off?" I said, "Yes, I did." Well, he said, "You know, you're a first lieutenant now but I think you might be better off being a private. A private *no* class." And I said, "Yes sir, yes sir, yes sir." What else could I say?

Alaskan Winter

Excerpt from *The Thousand-Mile War: World War II in Alaska and the Aleutians* by Brian Garfield

There were no trees—wind kept them from taking root. Here and there crouched a wind-stunted shrub. The inland valleys grew thick with rank weeks, coarse wild rye grass, ferns, parsnip, monkshood, fireweed, and other wildflowers that blazed forth brilliantly in summer. Beneath all this lay the muskeg—a thin elastic crust of matted dead grasses something like celery, overlying topsoil of dark volcanic ash which became quicksand whenever it was wet, which was to say all the time. The muskeg's spongy animus would prohibit the movement of men, jeeps, tanks, or airplanes; the mud would suck the boots off the infantrymen.

Dutch Harbor

They couldn't understand that you could be drunk and still keep track of the number of buckets.

The Soviets were our allies and I remember we used to have these old rusty boats of theirs come in to refuel. Some of the captains were women, five feet high and five feet wide, and they would bark these men around like nobody's business. I don't know if these ships were part of some joint effort with us. It didn't seem that way to me. If they were, they certainly hid their talents under a bushel basket. They were to get only so many buckets of coal, and I was in charge of keeping track of what they took. Well, they would ply me with vodka and more vodka, and of course I'd drink it. I would always have a pencil, and when five buckets were put into the hold, I would put a scratch on the bulkhead. After ten of those scratches, I knew that was fifty buckets, and so on. As it got to be 140, I would become very expansive. I'd act a little more drunk than I was, and I might have been drunk to start with. But when it got to 150, I got up and walked down the plank, and no more coal went in the hold. The Russians would be talking to themselves. "What the hell happened?" They couldn't understand that you could be drunk and still keep track of the number of buckets.

"Where do I think the future might be?"

I was older than a lot of the enlisted men, and I would continually think of other things, because it was quite confining. Long winters. I was saying to myself, "I certainly am not going to be in this forever, and what am I really going to do? Where do I think the future might be?" And I decided in early '42 that I would go into the service business. And that's what I did.

We were told to say that we were stationed at Box 1142.

My orders were to report to a secret post in Virginia, near Washington D.C. I actually lived in Washington. The post was in Fort Hunt National Park but we were told to say that we were stationed at "Box 1142."

There was an interrogation unit at 1142 but I was assigned to General Marshall's staff, putting together the order of battle for the German army—the red book. I was the captain in charge of the MIRS, Military Intelligence Research Section. This was about twenty young men, primarily German Jews who, because of their work there, got U.S. citizenship. I was almost thirty by then and they were young—nineteen, twenty, twenty-one. You had to really be on the ball to be in charge of them. They were so intelligent and they just absorbed knowledge like sponges. Fortunately, I had a great memory, which helped because we went over thousands of documents. Every day, we'd get big mailbags full of captured documents and we had to look through everything. If we found something that might have some useful information, we'd set it aside. We had to look at everything, tens of thousands of documents every day. Lots of them had no meaning at all but we had to look at everything and gather the information that went in the red book. This was the order of battle of the German army that went to General Eisenhower before D-Day.

I remember one document from a German colonel. This guy must have been a nutcase. He had a notebook of the various women he'd made love to—the location, the positions, even sometimes a clipping of her hair. And this guy had been very active. This was a whole book, and it was taken from my desk by somebody. I never found out who.

Previous spread: The Military Intelligence Research Section, Box 1142. Top row: Sgt. Bogdanov, Cpl. Rober, Cpl. Fairbrook, Lt. VanLoon, Lt. Snowwite, Lt. Kluge. Bottom row: Lt. Goldsmith, Lt. Brinkerhof, Lt. Thiemann, Lt. Rode, Lt. Herbeck

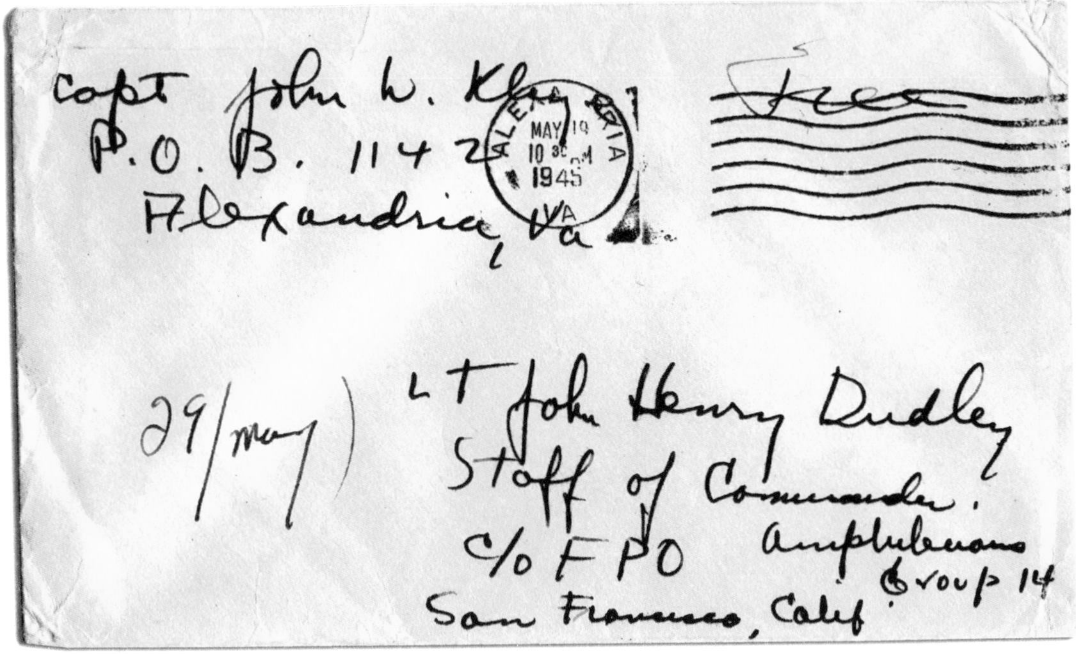

Capt John W. Kl[illegible]
P.O.B. 1142
Alexandria, Va

ALEXANDRIA MAY 19 10 30 AM 1945 VA

Free

29/May

Lt John Henry Dudley
Staff of Commander,
Amphibious Group 14
c/o FPO
San Francisco, Calif

With friendship
John

Spies
Interrogation

"We know you went to Rommel's daughter's wedding."

Besides the documents, we also had information we'd get through couriers or through spies. We would also follow the local newspapers, to find out who went where. And of course, we knew the chain of command. We had the telephone directory of the Reichstag, and we knew that 36 was a certain general and 45 was another general. Now, we'd get General 45 and we'd say to him, "Look, we got all that information between you and 36. We recorded it." Which we didn't. We just knew they'd communicated. We'd tell him, "We know you went to Rommel's daughter's wedding. We know. We had someone there and we saw you talking to General So-and-so." We didn't have anyone there, but it was in the newspaper, a list of the guests, and we surmised he'd be talking to this other general. We would make them think we had more information than we did, so they'd give us more.

July 13

Dear Dad

Hope this letter will get you at your old address or that it will be forwarded to you.

I was transferred about 65 miles from Washington, D.C. and today am getting orders to report again to a little station about twenty miles from the old town.

Wonder now just what you are doing. Hope you co get back within a year.

A Letter dated July 4th, 1945, from John Kluge to friend John Dudley:

I intend to learn Russian. They will share the world with us or do we share the world with them? ...

I don't have the "pep" and "push" I once had. And what concerns me is that I need more, you need more when we get back to the harness...

Still eager to work out some paper deal with you. By the way I have several good users lined up to sell them on a brokerage basis. Hope they don't give me the runaround. Some people are great on promises...

I was transferred about 65 miles from Washington D.C. and today am getting orders to report again to a little station about twenty miles from the old town...

You were working on their head.

When we'd interview these high-ranking prisoners, I'd laugh with them, joke with them. I'd let them think that I was maybe on their side. I played bridge with them—all this to kind of soften them up. And I'd drive them around Washington, give them believable misinformation. Give them bullshit. We'd pass the Pentagon and I'd say to these generals, "You know, this is just the annex. The Pentagon itself is underground and it makes this place look small." Well, you did all kinds of things with these people. You were working on their head.

To give you an example, we would know from past documentation who could understand English, who could speak English, and so on. Of course, they'd all say they couldn't speak English. If I was having trouble getting one of them to talk, one of the ones who understood English, I'd call in a man in a Russian officer's uniform. He was Russian, born in Russia, but he was an American officer. I would say to him, in English, "Look, we can't get any information out of this guy. We're going to give him one more day and if we still can't get him to tell us anything, I'm going to turn him over to you. You can send him to Siberia or do whatever you want." The Germans were deathly afraid of the Russians. *Deathly* afraid. So after that, things with the German went a lot better. It was amazing the way they'd open up.

KLUGE

We had the madams of these different places all sewed up.

We also had information from spies all through Europe. For example, there was an officer in one of the Panzer divisions in Italy who regularly visited the brothels. He'd get drunk and he'd spill his guts to the girls. Well, we had the madams of these different places all sewed up. You know, they were in our camp. We got every bit of information he ever gave them, and it corroborated other information we were getting about the path of that Panzer division. It all went into the red book.

I wanted to scare the hell out of him, and I did.

I lived in Washington, as I said, and one night I was dancing in the Blue Room at the Shoreham Hotel in Washington. Would you believe it, I bumped into the quartermaster from Dutch Harbor. I thought I'd give him something to worry about. I looked at him and I said, "I've told the president that you ought to stay in the Aleutians, and I'm certainly going to talk to him about it again tomorrow." And then we went right on dancing. I wanted to scare the hell out of him, and I did.

I heard the war was over.

I was standing right in front of the University Club on 16th Street and I heard the announcement. I knew I'd get out then. The army said, "Don't leave. We're going to make you a major." I said, "Thanks a lot, but I'll pass."

Washington, DC
Shoreham Hotel
Dutch Harbor
Quartermaster
US Army
University Club

Kluge in military uniform.

It's not how successful you are.

Did you do it without being either a con artist or a person who was so burned up with success that anything goes? I don't feel comfortable with "anything goes." Never have, never will.

John Kluge On Success

I haven't eaten Fritos since.

After the war, I was in the food brokerage business. I did that before I got into radio or television.

I visited Dallas, and I became a franchise holder of Fritos for New England. I established a plant, 678 Columbus Avenue, in Roxbury, Massachusetts. That first winter, I had one hundred broken axles. I rued the day I ever did this. Our distribution… well, it was pretty good but at that time Fritos were not packed in a sealed bag. Within fourteen days, the Fritos would get hard and lose their taste, or they'd be oily. So we all tried to get those Fritos out the door. I haven't eaten Fritos since.

I was the franchise holder for New England, from White Plains, New York, to Presque Isle, Maine. I got to know every little town in New England. I learned one thing: They didn't need anything. You couldn't sell them anything. I remember trying to sell Fritos to one buyer and he asked me if it was a new kind of shoe polish. I remember handing out samples in the store.

One night at about ten, Mr. Rabinowitz from Economy Stores, which became Stop 'N' Shop, came by the plant and said, "John, I signed a check this morning to your company." That remark gave me new encouragement because we really needed a check from somebody.

"That fellow is broke, but he doesn't know it."

At that time, one of my bankers was at Shawmut Bank in Boston. One day, he asked me to see him. I went in and said, "What do you want?" He said, "I just want to look at you. You move a million dollars in and a million dollars out of the bank in an hour, with a regular balance of $59." Later I asked for a loan, $5000, and he turned me down. I heard afterward that he said, "That fellow is broke, but he doesn't know it." Well, I didn't go bankrupt, and for many years I would have nothing to do with that bank.

Fleischmann's Yeast was one of my brands.

Besides Fritos, I added other lines: Kretchmer Wheat Germ, Endust, Woolite, Wrigley Gum, Bluebonnet Margarine. There are others, which I can't remember, and most of them were bought up by major companies.

Fleischmann's Yeast was one of my brands. After it was bought by Standard Brands, I met with the vice president. I remember he said, "John, you're doing a terrific job." I'd put them in ten thousand stores. I said, "You know, I'm going to do a better job for you. I'm going to drop five thousand stores." I thought he was going to have a stroke right then and there. But I said, "I want to tell you, that will give me more time to spend in stores that I know are going to make it—Stop 'N' Shop, First National." I could see that the mom-and-pop stores were on their way out and I wanted to focus on the others. The fellow putting foodstuffs on the shelves today, later on he might become an assistant manager and then a manager. When you work with him at a low level, then when he's the manager he trusts you. So I wanted to drop the smaller stores and spend my time on the others.

You know, the first week you do that, you worry. All of a sudden you don't have all these customers. But in the long run, you're going to be better off than sticking with the same old pattern. I like to keep reviewing what our objective is, what we're looking for as a result, and changes don't bother me. You know, it's supposed to be that one of the characteristics of getting old is that you don't want changes. I still welcome changes, I really do.

A fleet of Kluge's trucks ready to distribute the new Frito-Lay corn chips, c. 1950.

Opposite: Food broker John Kluge (far left, second row) visits the Frito-Lay plant, c. 1950.

I don't want any advertising.

I was the broker for International Silver Polish in the fifties. I brought them into supermarkets. A competing broker was talking to them, and they had 165 salesmen. When I went up to the International Silver Polish headquarters for the interview, they said to me, "How many salesmen do you have?" I said, "You're looking at him." Then they said, "Do you want a contract?" I said, "No, I don't want a contract." Evidently, this company that I was competing with wanted a five-year contract. I said, "Give me three months. If you don't like what I do, you can fire me." They said, "Well, what do you want in advertising?" I said, "I don't want any advertising. You think that a woman seeing an ad on television would run to the store to buy silver polish? She hates to polish silver. All I want you to do is put in back of each piece of silver, 'For best results use International Silver Polish.' And what I do want is a very attractive bottle. I want the silver polish to be lavender. And I want the label to be black with a white script, 'International Silver Product.'" They gave me the job.

I hired two or three girls to call brokers throughout the United States, everyone that I knew or had heard of, so I had the country covered. Then I put a man on the road and hired an office girl, and this girl was terrific on the phone. She had one of these voices that just—it clicked. I called it The Silver Company and I had it for fifteen years or so. When I dissolved that company, I had twelve million dollars in stocks.

I was a food broker until we sold the business sometime in the '80s but I'm still in on the food business today. Costco's private label nuts—walnuts and so forth—are from our company up in Kirkland, Washington. We also sell to Wal-Mart. We have steakhouses, and that's my favorite business because they're taking in money seven days a week.

My food business was based in Washington and my media business was based in New York. I would be in Washington in the morning, and in the afternoon I'd be in New York. I worked day and night, which didn't bother me actually.

Man on the Go

Excerpt from *Television Age*, April 15, 1963

"For instance, we advertised dill pickles in a local newspaper by getting the essence of dill into the printing ink so that people could smell it," he said. "It worked out pretty well. We sold more pickles than you could dream of. It was the first time they sold by the half-gallon. Somebody dropped a lot of the essence in the pressroom and they wouldn't talk to me for weeks at that paper."

Excerpt from *Food World*, May 1959

Predicting great opportunities for the young American businessmen, John Kluge, food broker and rising young industrialist, likened the youth of America to the young seals he saw while visiting the Pribilof Islands in the Bering Sea, S.W. of Alaska.

"Like young seals watching the old seals on Pribilof, they know that sometime or other they'll bump the old seal off and thereby gain control over the vast domains that were formerly held by the retiring leaders of another generation," Mr. Kluge told FOOD WORLD.

Getting set for a trip to Russia, in the middle of June, Kluge smilingly reflected for a moment, at his New York offices, when asked by Seymour Goodman, editor of the FOOD WORLD, for his three biggest thrills.

"As a German immigrant boy arriving in New York and looking around the great city was my first real thrill," said Kluge. "I suppose, two, was some time later while carrying my typewriter on the vast subterranean New York transportation system known as the subway; and thirdly, more recently, as I stood before the staff of Metropolitan Broadcasting corporation's WNEW, telling them I was glad to be on their team."

Kluge's WNEW finished the fiscal year with total sales of $14,500,000—a 40% gain over last year.

Above: "The site finally chosen after much searching. 'The land we acquired was a weird tract of property. Eleven acres at $1000 per acre, plus settlement fees.'"

Opposite: "Birth announcements of radio stations come from ordinary typewriters. Daddy Joseph Brechner is at left, Daddy John Kluge at right. Baby is WGAY."

You, Too, Can Own a Radio Station

Excerpts from *Saturday Evening Post*, January 25, 1947.

The article, written by Joe Brechner, describes how he and John got WGAY on the air in just over than a year. The biggest initial stumbling block was land. They had very specific needs as far as location and elevation, and real estate was at a premium as everyone anticipated the post-war building boom.

Predicting great opportunities for the week ends, John and I took pleasant hikes over the Maryland countryside, tramping over dirt roads in business clothes, looking for land. The winter of 1945-46 proved extremely sporting for us.... I was limited to week ends in helping John find a site. As a salesman he had a slightly more flexible schedule. During the week, he took cabs out into the countryside as far as he thought he could reasonably afford, and then he would hoof the rest of the way home.

[Eventually they located two adjacent plots that met their needs and made a deal with one owner. The other owner, a deeply religious widow, kept stalling. Finally, they ran out of time; the first landowner was about to leave on an extended vacation and they had to finalize the agreement before he left.]

The widow was uncertain and lonely. John spent long hours that evening in quiet conversation with her. He compared his army career with her son's, from peeling potatoes to cleaning latrines. He volunteered to dry the supper dishes and arranged the furniture. He put coal on the fire, praised her good taste in clothes and home furnishings. The agreement was yet unsigned, and midnight was approaching.

"Let's talk about it some other time," she said finally.

He talked faster and more furiously. At last, frustrated, he rose to leave. She didn't call him back. He returned voluntarily.

"You know," he said, "you remind me of my grandmother, who procrastinated about everything just as you do."

"What did she do about it?" asked the widow.

"She used to open up the Bible and read a paragraph. If it seemed to coincide with the thought in her mind, she was sure the Lord approved it."

"There's the Bible," she said, pointing to the mantelpiece. "Read something to me."

John swallowed hard when he reached for the Bible. He opened the book and his eyes glanced at a verse:

And they bend their tongues, like their bow for lies:
But they are not valiant for the truth upon the earth:...

He quickly turned to another chapter and read to himself:

His mouth is full of cursing and deceit and fraud:
Under his tongue is mischief and vanity.
He sitteth in the lurking places of the villages:
In the secret places doth he murder the innocent:...

The widow grew impatient. "Read me something!"

John turned to a blank page at the back of the book. He heard himself reciting an unprinted prayer from his own heart, "The Lord's ways are definite. Give us poor miserable beings strength and wisdom to follow Thy ways."

The widow leaned back, her eyes closed. When she reopened them, she said, "I'll sign."

Warmest
Greetings
At
Yuletide

Clockwise from top: WGAY offices; "Dolores Dupont on the air as WGAY's first 'live' entertainment gets underway" (original *Saturday Evening Post* caption); WGAY's first Christmas card.

KLUGE

Saturday Evening Post
WGAY
Qantas Airways
Australia
Joseph Brechner

96

I read that you could start a radio station for $15,000.

I knew Joe Brechner from Detroit. We were in high school together and Mrs. DaRatt helped him get his first full-time job. The same time I went to Otten Brothers, he went into commercial radio. After the war, we were both living in the DC area. I had the food brokerage and he was back in radio. In November 1945, I read an article in the *Wall Street Journal* that you could start a radio station for $15,000 so I called Joe. He said, "It's impossible," and he was right. Our corporation was capitalized by $50,000 and we spent every penny.

The prize was a one-way ticket to Australia for your mother-in-law.

We went on the air in December 1946—December the 7th, because that was a meaningful date. For weeks after, people would say to me, "You know, I like the music on your station but I hear a kind of hammering noise." And I always said, "Well, it must be your radio." But it *was* hammering, because we still weren't finished with the building.

Joe was the manager, and he was a very good manager. We'd do our own promotions, to create an interest. The most successful promotion we had was with Qantas Airlines. The prize was a one-way ticket to Australia for your mother-in-law. That was very popular.

Basically, I don't like business.

At the beginning, I said, "Joe, I'll get you advertisers and so on and so forth. But I don't really want to run a station." It may sound funny to you, but the reason I'm in a lot of businesses is that, basically, I don't like business. I would get very bored with one business. That isn't enough of a challenge for me. I know when you have one business you can make a challenge by making it international and all kinds of things, but it's still the same business. Over the years, I've been in and out of over two hundred businesses. I always wanted something new.

WGAY Promo cards.

Man on the Go

Excerpt from *Television Age*, April 15, 1963

"We had a community station [at WGAY]. It did an outstanding job. We felt that a community needed more than a station that just played records. I said from the start that we were going to weave ourselves into the community like an old country doctor. We did, supplying public service and interest."

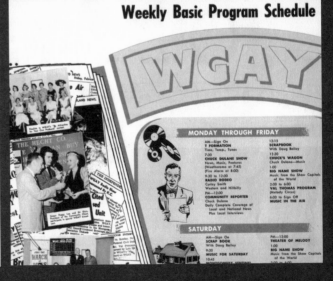

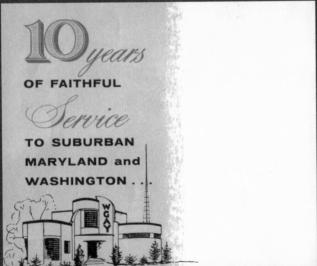

I like taking risks.

I guess it's like an addiction.
My addiction is taking a risk.

When you have nothing, why not take a risk? You can only fall on your face.

John Kluge On Risk

He would sign nearly every check, and you can't manage a company like that.

I think Alan DuMont was a great scientist. He was not a good CEO. He micromanaged. He would sign nearly every check, and you can't manage a company like that. And he was not a good marketer. For example, he sold only thousand-dollar television sets, when he should have put out a couple of hundred-dollar sets too—rough, tough, not fancy. People wanted to see the picture and they didn't care about a piece of furniture. But he was quite scientific, a real innovator, and if he had been a great marketer, he would have been *the* person in television. But you know, he got into financial trouble so they separated Alan DuMont Manufacturing from Alan DuMont Broadcasting, which became Metropolitan Broadcasting.

So I didn't found the company. What I did was change its operation entirely. Instead of being a company with a few relatively isolated outlets, I broadened it into a national company, in more than one medium—transit advertising, outdoor advertising, radio and television. I expanded into the entertainment business, movie and production companies, and the Ice Capades, the Harlem Globetrotters. I had a lot of energy in those days.

Timing is everything.

I felt the time was right for the independent stations to become more successful. And why? Because the ABC, CBS and NBC networks were strong and getting stronger. I felt as these stations became more successful, they would raise their rates which would give independent stations an umbrella. If I used what I learned early in my business years and kept tight financial controls, I could turn these stations around. And that's exactly what happened.

Alan DuMont
DuMont Television Network
Metropolitan Broadcasting
Frugality
Ice Capades
Harlem Globetrotters
Timing
Metromedia
Secaucus, New Jersey

That's how Metromedia got started.

On January 5th, 1959, I became chairman of the board of the television company. I wanted a name that was broad and encompassing and yet made some indication as to the core of our business. Broadcasting was only part of our business, and we focused on metropolitan areas, the big cities. I remember having a prolonged argument with one of the members of the board, an investment banker. He wanted "Metro Media" as a name. Capital M-e-t-r-o. Capital M-e-d-i-a. I said, "No. It's got to be one word."

That's how Metromedia got started. I operated as chief executive from the beginning of 1959 to the time I took the company private, in 1984.

We were always quite lean, because we had to be— we'd go broke otherwise.

I said we needed tight financial controls, and we had them, but we also wanted to make sure our office space was somewhat opulent. Being an independent, we didn't want to look like a poor cousin. I don't mind spending money if there's a reason for it. But we really did evaluate every move. For example, we moved to Secaucus many, many years ago, and we would transmit from New Jersey to New York. We never brought the film physically in to New York, because that saved us in taxes.

I felt that the networks were going to get richer and richer, and happier and happier, and fatter and fatter. We were always quite lean, because we had to be—we'd go broke otherwise. But as the networks became more and more successful, as independents, we could put our money back into programming and lift ourselves up by a bootstrap. That was certainly a challenge. It took a lot of years to do that, but we did.

With Cousteau, I went to him because at that time everybody was going to space. I said, "Let's go underwater."

Jacques Cousteau and his underwater research vessel, *Puerto Rico*, launched on New Year's Day 1960. Metromedia produced several episodes of *The Undersea World of Jacques Cousteau* during the 1960s and 1970s.

We counter-programmed.

The networks would have news at eleven; we'd have news at ten. In Washington, for example, the government workers all go to bed early. They don't want to wait till the eleven o'clock news, so that's why we introduced it at ten.

I introduced the ballet. I'd go to London and meet a guy in front of Harrod's and pay him cash for the film, then we'd fly it to New York. Because of the time difference, we were able to get the film the next day, or sometimes even the same day. It looked like we were connected. We did the same thing with the symphony, with the Royal Shakespeare Company. On the west coast we introduced tennis, which was very boring until we learned the techniques of videography.

We'd show movies. We'd have a whole week of Elizabeth Taylor, a whole week of Marlon Brando. If I had to do it all over again, I'd buy those libraries. We also created product, like Jacques Cousteau. I was partners with Jacques Cousteau for twelve years and we supported his research ship, the *Calypso*. You'll be interested in this: Jacques Cousteau would not eat fish.

We bought a lot of the syndicated shows, like *All in the Family*. You could play them over and over; if you had ten percent of the audience, then ninety percent of the people weren't seeing it but they might see it at a later time. Those shows are still on today, and syndication is a major part of programming.

We did some good market research.

But we also winged a lot of stuff. With Cousteau, I went to him because at that time everybody was going to space. I said, "Let's go underwater." See, we constantly counter-programmed.

I introduced bullfighting and I had to take that off immediately. We introduced wrestling, and you'd be amazed how many people like wrestling. You know, a lot of it's just fake, but it sure brings people to the screen.

KLUGE

Metromedia's New Home

Excerpt from *Radio Television Digest*, November 12, 1965

Gracious and sometimes opulent "at home" atmosphere is the current corporate trend in headquarters' furnishings. Pictured here, for example, are some of the highlights of Metromedia's new executive offices on New York's Park Avenue. The decorator tried for, and achieved, a warm feeling which all but ignored the Bauhaus school of design. Period furniture is mixed with the art collected by Metromedia chief John Kluge. Occasional accents (Ice Capades costume dolls and Foster & Kleiser posters) point up the diversification of Metromedia's varied interests. Photos are by Len Jossel.

Every time that damn mule got into the elevator, it would do its business.

We introduced a lot of different things—*Wonderama*, one of the earliest children's shows. It had a mule, and every time that damn mule got into the elevator, it would do its business.

We had personalities on like David Frost, Merv Griffin, David Susskind. I brought David Susskind down to my house in Washington for a party, and the FCC commissioners were there too. He didn't know anybody, and before I had a chance to introduce anyone, David said, "The FCC commissioners are the dumbest people in the world, and the dumbest of them all is the chairman"—and he's looking at him. But we worked it out.

Opposite: David Susskind.

We never knocked the networks. Never.

The networks, I think, saw us as sort of an upstart, kind of brash, but I think they respected us, because we tried to better the programming all along, and we made investments in building up the stations. We became more successful as they became more successful, and with the counter-programming, we were able to succeed and have very effective cost controls. We ran a profit-and-loss on every station, every week. We made controls on a weekly basis because if something wasn't working, we would change it.

We never knocked the networks. Never. No matter what they did, we always deferred to them. I learned early on. Before Metromedia, I owned a radio station in Tulsa, Oklahoma, and there was a 50,000-watt station that sold spots for two dollars. Well, how do you compete against that? You can't. So I learned you'd better be in a market where the rates are higher, so you can make a living.

KLUGE

Metromedia
Peter Max
Transit advertising
Media Decisions

110

Peter Max in Transit

Excerpts from *Media Decisions*, March 1969

Transit advertising will never be the same again. On March 30 about 22,000 buses will roll out of terminals in 10 cities as a traveling exhibition of pop artist Peter Max's work.

To the famous artist it's the most exciting thing he's ever done. His psychedelic designs will be exhibited almost simultaneously on the scene to millions of people in all stations of life.

"What artist in the past," he asks, "has ever had a chance to exhibit his own non-commercial art to the masses? The only message I'll convey will be my own expressions in visual symbols of peace, love, joy, evolution. I'll be able to bring lots of color to people in the big cities where there is too much chrome, cement, and plastic life. It's just fantastic. I'm jumping!" ...

Art exhibits are nothing new to Metromedia. John Kluge, president, has decorated almost all of the company's offices with the works of varied artists, some unknown, some among the greatest. A Rembrandt and a Picasso hang in the board room in New York.

When Kluge and Max met recently in Peter's studio, the rapport was immediate. Peter Max divides people into U-25's and O-25's, under and over 25 years old in outlook, regardless of age. He classifies Kluge as definitely U-25. The difference, says Max, is that the U-25ers are open minded; the O-25ers are closed.

I still believe that public service leads to making a station more responsible.

When I first went into broadcasting the FCC was much more oriented to public service. That's what we did. We would have so much public service, so much news, so much music. I still believe that public service leads to making a station more responsible. I think the deregulation that's been going on here for years has been carried too far. There is no question in my mind that diversity is good for the American public. When you have three or four people owning ninety percent of the radio stations, ninety percent of the television stations, you have limited voices. Their commercial interests supersede everything. If you don't have prescribed rules and regulations of public service, they will become crass commercial operations, which I think is what has happened. That's not good for the American public.

Educational television and educational radio are good, but there are many more stations that are commercial. If they have the responsibility, the public is better served. I know we have entertainment and we have news but, you know, we don't have anybody standing up for anything. The thing they stand up for is the almighty dollar.

KLUGE

Metromedia
Deregulation
Channel 13
Hollywood
Chicago Tribune
Ford Foundation
Education

We put up the first million dollars to get an education channel in New York.

Metromedia helped create Channel 13. As a matter of fact, we put up the first million dollars to get an education channel in New York. Then we got NBC, ABC, CBS, and the *Chicago Tribune* and General Tire and some others, and we got $6 million together. I saw the president of the Ford Foundation at the University Club, and I said, "This is the chance of a lifetime." I think they put up the other $7 million. But boy, it was hard to get everybody in.

I've always believed in education, and I felt that an education channel was important—a channel that didn't depend on ratings, didn't depend on anything but giving information or educational guidance to younger people, or even older people. It was just something I felt was important. I've always felt that education was a great opportunity in this country. If you don't do it early, you can't do it later on. It's too expensive. I think the whole price to start Channel 13 was $13 million. Do you know what Channel 13 would be worth today? Two-hundred-fifty million or more.

I think the government should have designated early on, in these major markets, an educational channel. I think the government should have said, when they set up the frequencies, "This is for education," so commercial interests couldn't get involved at all.

Kevin Costner (center) and Jim Wilson (left) won the Best Picture Oscar for 1990's *Dances with Wolves*, which they co-produced for Orion Pictures. Costner also won Best Director for the same film. Michael Blake won for Best Screenplay. The following year, Orion had another blockbuster hit and Oscar winner with *Silence of the Lambs*. Despite these successes, Orion declared bankruptcy in 1992.

Dances with Wolves
Orion Pictures
Hollywood
Michael Eisner
Jacques Cousteau
National Geographic

I strictly was in the background, and that's not how the movie business works. If it works.

I didn't want to go in the movie business. I helped a friend out, you know, and the next thing I knew we were $700 million dollars in debt and borrowing from the bank. In the movie business, they spend money like water. Michael Eisner was in New York and he came to the New York apartment. He said, "John, you don't understand Hollywood. Hollywood is a town of relationships." I said, "Yeah, Michael. You run out of money, you run out of relationships." That is one phony city.

I bought a production company, and we did all kinds of television. Jacques Cousteau, some of the *National Geographic* films. But, you know, they say the two best days in your life are the day you buy a boat and the day you sell a boat. Well, I want to tell you, with a movie studio, it's a great day when you buy it and when you sell it, you celebrate two days instead of one.

I never went to a movie party. I never went to the awards. I strictly was in the background, and that's not how the movie business works. If it works.

If you go to Times Square and you see those fashion girls and boys on the sides of buildings, we did that.

I got started in outdoor in 1960, when I bought Foster & Kleiser. Then I bought other companies and we became the largest national outdoor advertising company. I didn't want to be in rural areas or scenic areas, because you'd have to drive a long way to get to those boards and they paid the least amount of money. I wanted to be in industrial or business areas, and that's what we did.

Because of our cash flow, we were able to do the research for new technology. I'm telling you, we had a hard time doing it. It took five years and many millions of dollars, but we did it. We developed a way to print images on vinyl sheets, like a photograph, and you could hang those sheets outdoors. If you go to Times Square and you see those fashion girls and boys on the sides of buildings, we did that. We came out with that in 1987 and we marketed the service, not the system. And today we're still the leaders in the world of digitized graphics.

We developed new ideas in how to sell outdoor too. For example, in Los Angeles, we divided the city into eight different sections, so a smaller advertiser could take one section at a time and just rotate around the city. The large companies, automobile companies, beer companies—they could buy a complete showing. But I was more interested in developing outdoor for smaller advertisers.

KLUGE

Outdoor advertising
Foster & Kleiser
Billboards
Digitized graphics
Times Square
Los Angeles, California

John Kluge pictured with the revolutionary new technology developed by
Metromedia to produce spectacular graphics for outdoor advertising.

Above and opposite: John Kluge displays the dramatic and eye-catching graphics made possible by Metromedia's proprietary technology.

I didn't do a lot of research.

In the final analysis, you might have a body of facts, but do the facts really become meaningful to the consumer, the customer?

That's the reason I went into Ice Capades and Globetrotters. We used that vehicle as an entertainment vehicle, so if we were in Detroit we'd have all the automobile people come, with their grandchildren or children, and it gave a different feeling about Metromedia, as a company. The same with Globetrotters. There's sort of an off-key analysis, in the sense that it seems like it was far-fetched. But we ran it efficiently, and it made a few million dollars a year. And the impact of that company was greater than the company's business.

Above: Dorothy Hamill, gold medalist in figure-skating at the 1976 Olympics. She performed with the Ice Capades the following year, and here she puts a last-minute touch to the hairdo that sent thousands of girls rushing off to the hairdressers in search of the "wedge."

Following spread: In one of their signature crowd-pleasers, Harlem Globetrotters Freddie Neal (left) and Meadowlark Lemon pass a spinning basketball back and forth on their fingers.

121

White tiger
Publicity

For that $10,000, we got a million dollars in goodwill.

I've always paid attention to that sort of thing. In 1960 we gave a white tiger to the National Zoo. I bought her from the Maharajah of India, and her name was "Mohini," which means "The Enchantress" in Hindi. I got criticized for spending so much money. She cost $10,000, you know. But for that $10,000, we got a million dollars in goodwill.

After the donation to the National Zoo, Metromedia put together an impressive, zebra-bound scrapbook including photographs of Mohini and clippings from every newspaper and magazine that carried the story of the white tiger.

I paid $5 million a week in interest. The bank used to call me to see how I was feeling.

My philosophy always was to build a company and not worry about the price of the shares. In fact, I did a number of things which might have hurt the shares but helped the company, long-term. But one day Metromedia stock went down to the twenties, which was the price it had been years before. I felt if the market didn't appreciate what was going on, I may as well take the company private so then I could do what I wanted to do, without thinking in terms of the stock at all. I got some criticism—that I took the company private and made many millions in doing so. That was never the driving purpose. The driving purpose was the stock didn't get recognition, and I felt it deserved recognition. That's why I took it private. It was a function of the stock. And no stockholder who stayed with the company ever, ever suffered.

And taking Metromedia private—that was the biggest risk I ever took. I certainly didn't make millions right away. I had to borrow, personally, a billion three hundred million dollars. The interest rate shot up to 20 percent, and I paid $5 million a week in interest. The bank used to call me to see how I was feeling. I used to have a lot of modern art—Jackson Pollock, Kandinsky—I had to sell those. I had to sell real estate to keep afloat. But, you know, interest finally came down, I was able to refinance and then I sold parts off to different people, and then I sold it all to Rupert Murdoch.

I just sold the whole thing to Rupert and we saved a billion dollars in taxes doing that.

One of the reasons I sold out to Rupert Murdoch was because of double-taxation legislation. If you sold an asset you'd pay a tax, and if you sold the whole company you'd pay another tax on top of that. So I just sold the whole thing to Rupert and we saved a billion dollars in taxes doing that.

But the other reason was, I was ready for something new. I wanted to focus on cell phones. You know, it was my attorney who got me into this, in 1980. I was walking into a hotel barroom in Washington for a luncheon and he said, "John, you ought to be in cellular radio." That's what he called it. I said, "What's that?" He said, "I'll send you some stuff."

When I read it, I took my top employees and I said, "Look, the next sixty days, this is all you're doing." We went into these cellular phones in a big way. We put in applications everywhere we could, and we spent $300 million we didn't have. Well, it started as 300 million and it went to five and a half billion. But I figured that the American people, who always are on the go, would want to have a phone with them wherever they were, the young people especially. Just on that simple belief, I went. I didn't study it. I just felt it. And today it's very much a reality.

If we had had more time we would have put more applications in. Still, we were able to get New York, Boston, Chicago, Washington, Dallas, Los Angeles, a few other areas. I think it became profitable immediately. And of course it has had an international impact.

Rupert Murdoch
Bloomingdale's
New York Post
Power

Rupert's really not interested in money. He's interested in power.

When Rupert Murdoch went to Bloomingdale's to get them to advertise in the *New York Post*, the president of the company said to him, "Your readers are our shoplifters." Well, CBS used to say, "Sure, Metromedia has a viewership but they're all second-class citizens."

I like Rupert Murdoch because he's not a white shoe. You might not agree with his philosophy—he's kind of conservative—but Rupert's really not interested in money. He's like Armand Hammer. He's interested in power.

He knows what he wants, and he's willing to pay for it.

Would you believe that when Rupert Murdoch came here from Australia, he said to me at lunch one day, he said, "I've got $4 million. I'm afraid to put it in a bank in New York because, as you know, the banks are shaky."

The thing I like about Rupert Murdoch is that he knows what he wants, and he's willing to pay for it. I'll tell you, he bought our independent stations for $2 billion. I had to wait until he became a US citizen, because the license has to go to a US citizen. I remember Rupert and I were walking down 42nd Street, and he said, "You know, Drexel Burnham wants $100 million for the transaction."

I said, "Well, Rupert, I'll tell you. You'll receive about $50 million. Don't go with the deal. But I'll give you the $50 million, and I'll make the deal." And that's what we did. We saved a lot of money on legal fees.

When I sold Orion, I called up Rupert first. What I like about him is that he doesn't say, "Send me the material. My people and I will look it over." He gives you an answer right over the phone. No, he wasn't interested. So MGM bought Orion. Rupert is very direct, and for a seller, that can be very important.

KLUGE

Metromedia
Rupert Murdoch
MGM
Orion Pictures
New York Times
Aging

132

Why limit the dream to what your life expectancy is?

A few years ago, the *New York Times* quoted one of the bankers saying that I'm the only 90-year-old that has a 30-year time vision. I don't mean to imply that I'm going to live forever, because I'm not, but why limit the dream to what you think your life expectancy is?

For example, somebody wrote, almost fifteen years ago, that we should be out of the video business. We're still in there. We used to get in laser discs before; now it's DVDs. We're in the medical field, the energy field, the restaurant field, we're in the beauty field. We're in the technical field of lighting—television screens, medical monitoring systems. Altogether, sixteen businesses now.

I am involved, but not on a daily basis. I tell you, I don't make notes. When I have a telephone conversation with New York for an hour, let's say, I have to keep it all in my head. I don't make notes purposely. I never made notes in college because I found out if I make notes, I don't have it in my head and I have to refer to the notes. You heard about the fellow who went four years to college, and on his way home he lost his notebook, so he had to go back another four years. Well, I didn't want to be that fellow.

I don't think about my age.

My age doesn't mean a thing. If I have my health, you can say I'm fifty. So far I've had my health, or I've been able to overcome any physical problem. I travel a little, but not much. I have the facts in my head, and I love to play with them. And until I broke my hip, I would travel all over the world. China, to Russia, to Georgia, Latvia, you name it. I don't travel as much anymore. But I go to California and I go to, of course, New York. And the hip doesn't really bother me except I use a cane now because of equilibrium. I don't feel old.

You know, in 1980, I was sixty-six and I owed more money than I ever owed in my life. And I made more progress between sixty-six and eighty-five than I ever made before that. I don't think about my age.

If I like something, I buy it.

I'm a collector because I enjoy looking at art. If I like something, I buy it. I brought art into our company because I wanted our employees to feel that it was not just a place of business. And I collect poster art, I collect modern art, ancient art. I like Henry Moore, I like Miró. The front doors at Morven, the farm in Virginia, were the last work of Miró. Giacomo Manzú did the doors at St. Peter's Basilica in Rome, and I asked him if he'd do a set of doors for me. He thought it over and after a few months he said no because he felt that was sacrilege. So I asked him to do a fireplace. Yes, he'd love doing a fireplace. I asked Miró if he would do a set of doors. Sure, he'd do a set of doors.

I went through a period back in the '60s, collecting California artists and California crafts. They were in woodworking, in ceramics, in weaving, as well as painting and sculpture. But the Eastern establishment was more oriented to the European art. It wasn't as big, and space in New York is expensive. They couldn't collect these California people, and therefore they didn't promote them.

I've had various sculptures—eighteen by Maillol. Some by Rodin, Henry Moore, Robert Graham, Monzú, Pomodoro, and there were others. I bought horse paintings by English painters, and primitive paintings. Sixth and eighth century ceramics. Bronzes from 5000 B.C. to 400 A.D.

I'm not what you call a very talented collector. I never buy because I'm going to make money on the art. There have been certain artists that I follow, that I collect as a way of supporting their work. I did that over a period of time with Robert Graham, Robert Rauschenberg, a number of artists I believed in. Today I'm really not interested in collecting any more. In fact, I'm selling art because I have too much of it. I asked the curator how many pieces I had of furniture and art. He said 20,000. And I thought to myself, "It's time to get rid of some of this stuff."

KLUGE

Clockwise from top: La Riviere by Aristide Maillol (1861-1944); Colossal Roman marble of Septimius Severus, 200-210 AD; *Four Seasons: Winter*, late 17th century, Belgium; *La Nuit*, Maillol; *Figure in Shelter* by Henry Moore (1898-1986); *Figure in Shelte*r, side view. The Maillol sculptures are part of a suite of eighteen, also held by the Louvre.

I commissioned whole tribes to give their history in art.

I went to the Northern Territory in Australia different times and commissioned whole tribes to give their history in art. I gave fifteen hundred pieces of Aboriginal art to the University of Virginia, and I gave them my curator of Aboriginal art, and she does a fabulous job traveling with it, writing about it. She's a real student of Aboriginal art.

John Kluge first became interested in Aboriginal art in the 1980s and soon became one of the genre's major collectors. In 1993, he purchased the collection and archives of the late Professor Edward L. Ruhe of Lawrence, Kansas. Ruhe began collecting and researching Aboriginal art while visiting Australia as a Fulbright Scholar in 1965. Kluge donated both collections to the University of Virginia, and today the Kluge-Ruhe Aboriginal Art Collection is recognized as one of the finest in the world.

Previous spread: Namarnkol the Barramundi by Yirawala, ca. 1965. Natural pigments on eucalyptus bark.

Right: Stingray Hunting Story, Nakaramba, 1961, Natural pigments on eucalyptus bark

Opposite: Mimih dancers by Paddy Compass, Namadbara, c. 1965, Natural pigments on eucalyptus bark

I was never rooted to a place. I was rooted in ideas.

I never had much roots, so to speak. I came to this country at the age of eight, I left home at fourteen, and I've made my way ever since. So I haven't had the privilege of being in a home with a grandfather and grandmother and a sense of being rooted there. I never was rooted to a place. I was rooted in ideas that I had but not to anything in any physical way. I happen to be a very private person, and I need a lot of time alone. That doesn't mean I don't like people. I do like people. But I need space, and I like to be completely private if I can be. Privacy is not easy to get, especially these days.

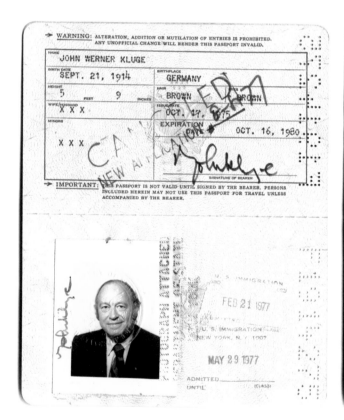

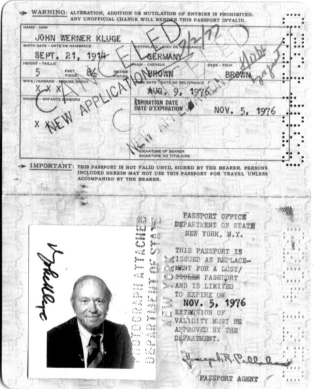

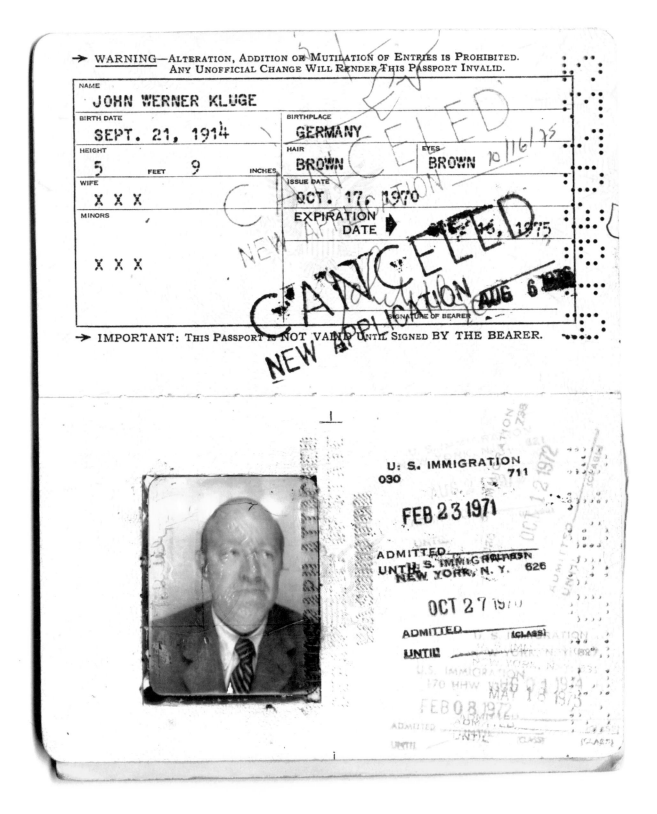

→ WARNING—ALTERATION, ADDITION OR MUTILATION OF ENTRIES IS PROHIBITED. ANY UNOFFICIAL CHANGE WILL RENDER THIS PASSPORT INVALID.

NAME
JOHN WERNER KLUGE

BIRTH DATE
SEPT. 21, 1914

BIRTHPLACE
GERMANY

HEIGHT
5 FEET 9 INCHES

HAIR
BROWN

EYES
BROWN

WIFE
X X X

ISSUE DATE
OCT. 17, 1970

MINORS
X X X

EXPIRATION DATE → ___ ___, 1975

SIGNATURE OF BEARER

CANCELED
NEW APPLICATION

→ IMPORTANT: THIS PASSPORT IS NOT VALID UNTIL SIGNED BY THE BEARER.

U. S. IMMIGRATION
030   711
FEB 23 1971
ADMITTED
UNTIL U.S. IMMIGRATION
NEW YORK, N.Y.   626
OCT 27 1970
ADMITTED   (CLASS)
UNTIL
FEB 08 1972

141

We've set a rule in our companies: No family.

The three or four most important principles of business ethics? I think honesty. I think the ability to make people feel they're part of the company, which is like owning a part of the company. I think thirdly the chief executive has to be modest in his wishes, in his salary, in his deportment. And fourthly he has to give people an opportunity, whether sending them to school or making his employees feel like they will have a chance for advancement. We've set a rule in our companies: no family. Because if you allow it, you can't employ the best people.

KLUGE

Business ethics
Honesty
Metromedia
Excess
FTC

142

Ethics has to come from the front office.

I think the day that a business doesn't have ethics is the day that spells out ruin for the business. Because it's criminal. You might get away with one, or two, or three robberies. But eventually you get caught. Well, if a company has poor ethics, eventually they will be discovered. Ethics has to come from the front office. They have to provide the leadership. If they don't have the leadership, the company will play loose also.

When I ran a public company, I always felt it was not my company; I'm working for these people called shareholders. I bought my own lunch and my own car. The gall of people in corporate life! I had Ken Lay down here, and he came down with four people. All I remember is him talking about what connections he had in Washington, what connections he had in the capitals of different states. He made me very nervous, in part because the people I asked advice from were just different people. They knew right from wrong, and most people do know right from wrong. I was very naive in a lot of ways, but I wasn't naive about being fair.

You know, today there's a big movement on to get friends of the company chairman or CEO off the boards, because they don't really look at what's happening in the company. The president takes good care of his friends on the board and they take good care of him. It's like a club. That's not the way I am. It has nothing to do with being a goody-goody, but it does have something to do with ethics.

I honestly believe too many chief executives live off the company. Actually, they're living off their other stockholders, and I'm amazed that a lot of the chief executives hold very little stock. We've been going through a period where the public institutions such as the FTC and the attorney general's office are starting to do something about it, but human nature being what it is, 25 years from now they'll be doing the same thing.

The important thing is to have power but never use it.

The minute you use power, you lose something. You lose other people. They might not react outwardly, but inside they'll react.

John Kluge On Power

I knew he'd do a good job.

Al Johnson was with me since 1947, and he handled the accounting. He'd do the financial reports and I'd sign off on them, even though I didn't see this stuff. I knew he'd do a good job. One night, he called me at about eleven and woke me up. He said, "John, I overwrote the checking account by a hundred thousand dollars." I said, "Al, you overwrote it, you figure it out," and I went back to sleep. I don't worry about those things.

If people are treated right, you'd be amazed how they respond.

People don't work for me; they work *with* me. I hate to give orders. I've gotten hundreds of letters from people who said the best years they ever spent in their business career were when they were at our company.

I guess the best way to describe it is that I like to do things in an oblique way, and if that doesn't work, I can get tough as hell. If it's necessary, I have no problem with that—none. I also have no problem firing somebody if I know they just can't make it. But it's not something I want to do. I don't find delight in doing it.

And if someone does their job, we don't interfere, ever. And I tell you, if people are treated right, you'd be amazed how they respond. People basically want to do a good job. People basically want to be helpful. And why should you, because of a few cases, rule with an iron hand? That makes the whole organization nervous. If someone needs to go, then you go through the right process. You make your case and people will agree that that fellow should be out. They themselves will understand why it had to happen, and that avoids disruptions.

In other words, you have to be fair. And if you err, it's better to err on the side of fairness rather than being authoritative. The important thing is to have power but never use it. The minute you use power, you lose something. You lose other people. They might not react outwardly but inside, they'll react.

KLUGE

Working with people
Fairness
Television Age
Al Johnson
Micromanaging

146

Man on the Go

Excerpt from *Television Age*, April 15, 1963

"We have a willingness to make decisions and we have people who are willing to take responsibility," explains Mr. Kluge, applying his personality to the overall Metromedia concept. "We back our people up. Even if they make mistakes. We all make mistakes sometimes."

The Kluge attitude has indeed permeated the organization.... It is not uncommon for Bennett H. Korn, president of Metromedia's tv arm, Metropolitan Broadcasting Television, or Jack Lynn, the chief of programming, to close a half million dollar deal on their own—and only get around to letting Mr. Kluge in on it some time later.

"Good people help growth," Mr. Kluge sums up. "The executive who does everything works at the lowest common denominator. He also travels life's hypotenuse, the shortest distance between cradle and grave. I do as much inductive thinking as possible and I keep up by probing deeply here and there. I don't fly blind. I have my indicators."

Mr. Kluge feels that growth is possible only by encouraging executives within the company to take responsibility and keep making moves. He is proud of the profit-sharing plan and of the way the company's 1,692 employees are made privy to the company's progress. "I don't believe in just giving employees a gold watch after 25 years when, during that period, you haven't even given them the right time."

Craig Shergold and a small portion of the millions of cards he received from around the world.

I thought, "Well, a card is all well and good but could he be getting better care?"

In 1988, there was a boy in England, Craig Shergold, who had a terrible brain tumor in a spot that made it hard to operate. He was very sick and to cheer him up, they said, "Well, you've been getting a lot of cards so why don't you try to get the most cards ever and get yourself in the *Guinness Book of World Records*." The press over there started covering him and then people all over the world heard about it and he got millions of cards. I heard about him from a friend who wanted me to send Craig a card. I thought, "Well, a card is all well and good but could he be getting better care?" I talked to a doctor at the University of Virginia and he said there were some new instruments and treatments here that might help the boy. I told the doctor to let the Shergolds know that there was someone here in the United States who would pay for their passage and all the medical bills. I wanted to keep it anonymous. Well, the doctor didn't know how to reach them by telephone so he sent an express letter and of course it landed in the mailbag with all these other cards and letters. I think the record was just over a million letters, and he got millions and millions, you can imagine.

Anyway, the doctors told his parents that the chemotherapy hadn't worked and the tumor was growing again.

They said, "Take him home and make him comfortable because he's going to die." The next morning, Mrs. Shergold reached into the mailbag and found the doctor's letter. So we brought him here, to the University of Virginia Hospital, and they operated on him. I didn't want to see him. His hopes, the family's hopes, were raised and if he died after all this, I would feel very badly about that.

Well, they operated on him. It took more than five hours and it was a complete success. The university called me to come over there when he was leaving. They had a camera and all this sort of thing. I sat with him, and he said to me, "Mr. Kluge, I want to thank you for my life." Do you know what? I actually broke out in tears.

If I had to do it all over again, I would be in medical science.

I had Craig on my boat in London a few years ago. He lives at home, and his father and mother are just grateful that he's living. My birthday and Christmastime, I get cards from them, and they are effusive with their gratitude.

But that's when I thought to myself, "This is the field I should have been in." I have no regrets but if I had to do it all over again, I would be in medical science. With my competitiveness, which is inbuilt, I would have looked for a breakthrough somewhere. In other words, just being a scientist is nothing. It's the effort you put into the project to come up with a solution. And the medical field is a great area to be in.

About that time, I started funding cancer research. I'm still in it, and diabetes and sepsis. I'm going to tell you now that we're going to be successful in sepsis.

A note to John Kluge, Jr., from the Shergolds.

The Boy and the Billionaire

Excerpts from *Reader's Digest*, October 1991

By JOHN PEKKANEN

Craig Shergold and his father, Ernie.

[In 1989, young Londoner Craig Shergold was diagnosed with inoperable brain cancer. While in the hospital, he received so many cards from friends and loved ones that his doctor joked that he should try to break the world record. Soon the campaign to support Craig took off and people around the world began sending cards and letters. One of the people who took note of the boy's situation was John Kluge.]

As Kluge considered mailing a card, an inexplicable feeling came over him. Amid all the attention focused on the card campaign, he couldn't help wondering: Had every medical possibility been explored? Was there some treatment he could arrange for the boy? ...

Kluge phoned a close friend, Dr. Neal Kassell, professor of neurosurgery at the University of Virginia Health Sciences Center. "Neal," he said, "could you contact the Shergold family? I hve the feeling something important might have been overlooked. I'll pay any expenses."

Unable to reach the Shergolds by phone, Kassell air-expressed a letter.... Days passed, and the Shergolds did not answer. His letter, of course, had disappeared into millions of others.

[Looking for comfort and consolation, Craig's mother Marion decided to read some of her son's letters. The first envelope she picked up was the one from Dr. Kassell, and soon the family was on its way to Virginia. On March 1, 1990, Craig underwent five hours of surgery—which removed all traces of the tumor.]

A few weeks later, John Kluge came to the hospital to meet the Shergolds. When the businessman entered the room, Marion grasped his hand and thanked him. "You are our guardian angel," she said.

Kluge handed Craig a two-headed quarter. "This way," he said, grinning, "you'll never lose."

I've never liked the establishment because I'm not interested in the status quo. As a matter of fact, change is what I really like.

I'm not attached to things. I have things and I like them but if I lost them, I would still feel happy inside myself. In that respect, I'm a revolutionary.

John Kluge On Change

Ronald Reagan (left) and
John Kluge (center right).

Kluge and Hillary Clinton.

Kluge and Bill Clinton.

Ronald Reagan
Bill Clinton
Eleanor Roosevelt
Richard Nixon

Eleanor Roosevelt

I knew Eleanor Roosevelt. She was going to give us a weekly political commentary but then she died. But while we were negotiating that, I drove her over to the UN, to see Senator Adlai Stevenson, who was then representing us there. An aide of his came down and said he was on the floor and he'd be with us in ten or fifteen minutes. The aide left and Eleanor Roosevelt turned to me and said, "Wake me up in ten minutes." And with that she absolutely fell asleep. In fact, I kept looking at her because I thought she had died. I never saw anything like it. She was quite a woman.

Richard Nixon

I knew Nixon, and he was a very good international president. He was a poor domestic president but our foreign policy, between Nixon and Kissinger, was some of our best at that time.

Ronald Reagan

I admired President Reagan. You know, history is written many years later, and I think history will be kind to him.

Bill Clinton

Bill Clinton, well, he's very natural. Very relaxed. If he walked into this room, I don't care if you're a Republican or a Democrat, he would charm you like you can't believe. He could charm the birds out of the trees. Compared to JFK's personal charisma, I think his was greater. Clinton's was greater. Kennedy actually was quite shy. Not Bill Clinton.

Eisenhower with Mohini, the white tiger donated
by Metromedia to the National Zoo.

Dwight Eisenhower
Bob Hope
Harry Truman

Dwight Eisenhower

When I gave the white tigress to the National Zoo, there was a presentation with President Eisenhower on the White House lawn. I remember the president asked me, "Is she a Democrat or a Republican?" The Maharajah's castle was white, and the tigress looked over and saw the White House and she thought she was at home. She let out a tremendous yelp. Eisenhower turned to me and said, "Never mind." He had his answer. I liked him very much. He had a great personality. He didn't act like a general. He was very alert, and a person you'd like to know better.

Harry Truman

I knew Harry Truman, and of course he's is more respected as time goes on. He was very decisive. We used to interview him every year, after he left the White House. He lived in Independence, Missouri, you know. He had a house that was sort of "sugar," with a lot of fancy woodwork on the porches and so forth. He loved to play poker. They say he stayed in too many pots he should have gotten out of. I don't know.

Bob Hope

When you live to be my age, it's amazing how many people you get to know. I can tell you, Bob Hope—whom I knew—said, "If you want to feel old, stick with people older than you." He's right, and I've never done that. I've always been in businesses where there were young people—radio, television, telecommunications, the restaurant business—and my mind is young, I think young. Bob also said, "When your candles crush the cake, that's when you feel old." He's gone now, of course.

FRANK SINATRA

October 19, 1988

Dear John,

You must have a wall full of honorary degrees
by now, my friend; and nobody deserves the
recognition more than you. How marvelous
that the president and Trustees of Columbia
University will honor you on October 19.

You have always been a good and dear friend;
and Barbara and I love you. Our congratulations
to you and the wonderful people gathered to
salute you.

God bless,

Francis Albert

Mr. John W. Kluge
c/o Columbia University
Office of University Ceremonies
202 Low Memorial Library
New York, New York 10027

Frank Sinatra

Frank Sinatra was probably one of the most generous people I ever knew, and I knew him for many, many years. Down and out entertainers, charities he believed in—he would help and do it anonymously. He had his faults. He had a very hot temper. You could anger him very quickly. I saw that but I never got in any argument with Frank. But he was a pussycat in many ways. If you were his friend, he couldn't do enough for you. And of course, I think he was the greatest entertainer as a singer.

I was with Frank in Egypt when he performed before the pyramids. A lighting company from London came over to light up the pyramids, and it was dramatic. During his performance, Frank turned and looked at the pyramids and suddenly he lost his words. The audience supplied them. I said to Frank afterwards, "What happened?" He said, "When I looked back and saw the pyramid, I just blanked out. They were so overpowering." Which they are.

I bought his house on Beaumont in Beverly Hills, sight unseen. I told the realtor, "I don't have time to go see it, and I don't need to. If it's good enough for Frank, it's good enough for me." Later, when he married Mia Farrow, he wanted it back. I didn't want to sell but I did.

Frank was one year younger than I. When he died, my wife and I flew out to the funeral. Every seat in the church was taken and all the old stars were there. Sophia Loren, Tony Bennett, Angie Dickinson, you name it. If there's such thing as a beautiful funeral, that was it.

The Beatles

We brought the Beatles to Cleveland the first time. We hired a ten-thousand seat hall, but we got a hundred thousand requests. So we had to hire IBM to develop a reduction formula to ten thousand. Brian Epstein, who was the Beatles' promotional manager, would even sell their bed sheets. An eight-inch square for a dollar. I didn't think they were that great when I saw them come trudging out on *Ed Sullivan*. I thought they had no show quality at all. But then they simply captured the minds and hearts of the young people.

Tony Bennett

I've known Tony Bennett for nearly fifty years, and I told him, "You know, Tony, the thing that really impresses me is you haven't changed since the first day I met you. You haven't changed at all." And he hasn't. He's a painter, you know. His painting name is his given name, which is Benedetto. He was a painter before he was ever a singer. Tony Bennett is more attractive today than he was before.

John Kluge (far right) with Ethel Merman (far left),
Tony Bennett (second from left), and an unidentified friend.

Michael Jackson

I had Michael Jackson down to the house in West Palm Beach. I think he's a fabulous entertainer. He looked around and he saw the Maillols on the grounds. If you go to the Louvre, I have those same eighteen statues. Michael Jackson looked at them and he said, "What catalogue did you buy these out of?" But I think he's a fabulous entertainer, and I told him so. When he was visiting, my son John was here with another little boy—they were about ten years old at the time. I said to them, "I have some people visiting here I'd like you to meet." Oh, they didn't want to. They wanted to go out and play. I said, "Do me a favor." So they did. I introduced them to different people, business people and so forth, and that didn't mean a thing. Then I introduced them to Michael Jackson. Their eyes got big, you know. Junior's friend, Michael put his hand on his head and the boy said, "I'm never going to wash my hair!" Michael Jackson just sent him into the clouds.

Dalai Lama

The week after Michael Jackson, I had the Dalai Lama visit—two different personalities. I asked the Dalai Lama who his greatest teacher was. You know what he said? "The Chinese." They taught him to be patient. They taught him to try to understand their position. They taught him a lot of things, even though they were his enemies.

Andy Warhol

I knew Andy Warhol very well, and I knew how he did his art. Well, with a roller, and young kids doing it for him. One day I had lunch with Andy and he said, "You ought to go up to so-and-so gallery." He said that Jamie Wyeth did a portrait of him, and he did one of Jamie Wyeth. I bought the one that Wyeth did of Andy, but I didn't buy the one Andy did.

Gina Lollobrigida

I know Gina Lollobrigida very well. After she left show business she went into photography, and she's an excellent photographer. She did a book of photographs of Italy, *Mia Italia*. I think she's done more since.

I have to tell you a story about her. When the Apollo 11 astronauts got back from the moon and were traveling around the world, she entertained them at her place on the old Appian Way. One of the astronauts said, "Gina, I'll come back after a while." Well, she waited and waited, and finally he called and said, "Gina, I can't find your place. I lost my way." She said, "What? You find your way to the moon and you can't find my villa?"

She liked to see important people. She went to see Castro, and she had a diamond Piaget watch and he kept looking at it. He was wearing a steel Seiko watch. She said she saw that he was eyeing her watch, so she said, "Look, I'll trade watches." Of course, he said yes. She told him, "But I want you to engrave on the back of it, 'To Gina, with love, Fidel.'" So you know that watch is worth a lot today.

I had an apartment in the Waldorf Towers for 25 years, and she asked me if she could stay there for a weekend in August. No problem. Well, she stayed there a month. She took all the family pictures off the piano and put her own pictures on there, then held a news conference. She's a piece of work.

KLUGE

Gina Lollobrigida
Fidel Castro
Armand Hammer
Communism

162

Armand Hammer

Armand Hammer was more interested in power than money. I liked Armand. He and I used to travel the world together. Armand had his faults—which we all have—but I liked him. He was not particularly interested in money and he just was a driving force.

Armand would call me from all over the world, never figuring out what time it was on the other end. It might be four o'clock in the morning, you know. Armand was, especially in the later part of his life, very interested in eradicating cancer. And he always wanted Russia and the United States to eventually become friends.

Now, in my estimation, he was never a Communist. His father was a Communist, as well as a doctor, and Armand went to Columbia Medical School. He received an honor at Columbia and I talked to several of his classmates who were there. Armand came to the graduation in a Rolls Royce. Supposedly the money came from his father's pharmacy, where they sold a tonic which was made of eighteen percent alcohol or something like that. This was during Prohibition, and it was sold as a health tonic. It certainly made people feel better, especially old ladies.

Seawell

I don't like any publicity, to tell you the truth. If I've done a good job, I'll know it and I'll be happy with that. I don't need the publicity or the recognition. I like to see results, but without a lot of fanfare.

John Kluge On Publicity

It looked like I might make a good minister.

When I was a boy, I was a very good student and it looked like I might make a good minister, and I was offered a scholarship. I went to my minister's house with my friend, who was Catholic. I asked the minister a very simple question: Would my friend go to heaven? And the answer was, "Well, yes, he might. But it will be harder for him because he's not Lutheran." I made up my mind right then and there that I would never become a minister. That was that.

John Kluge with Pope John Paul II.

KLUGE

Religion
Lutheran Church
Fundamentalism
Roman Catholic Church

166

I would hate to think we are the final authority.

I strongly believe there is a power beyond ourselves. I would hate to think we are the final authority. You know, a belief is not based on a rationale. For example, when people declare themselves as atheists, they are actually using themselves as a final authority. I can't. I would feel very uncomfortable to be an atheist and declare myself as one. And I think part of that came from the fact that I belonged to a Lutheran church and went to a Lutheran parochial school, and I think it inculcated a sense of religion when I was younger.

I am a believer, and I will always be a believer. But I don't carry it on my sleeve. And I don't care whether you are a Catholic or a Jew or a Muslim. I don't care, as long as you have a feeling that there's an authority higher than yourself. There seems to be an idea that when you believe in something higher than yourself, then you don't understand the sophisticated world. There's nothing sophisticated about believing, but without it I think you're a very sad human being. You know people who have to tell you first thing that they're atheists. They want you to know that they are in control. I'm not very impressed, and I feel sorry for that person.

I think one's relationship to God is a very private thing. And I honestly believe that how I approach it is not the only way. I guess I'm the opposite of a fundamentalist. I think fundamentalism is wrong no matter where it is, whether it's in this country or in Iraq. They tend to be dangerous people because they're sure that what they believe is the only thing to believe. Everybody else is wrong.

Maybe I'm dreaming, but I just don't see fundamentalism in this country going beyond the [George W.] Bush presidency. I think basically the American people tend to be religious but not fundamentalist. Fundamentalism is very inflexible, and that's not what I see growing in this country.

It always comes down to fairness, putting yourself in somebody else's shoes.

We don't have a policy as much as we have managers who act responsibly in hiring minorities. We also fire them if they're no good. You'd be amazed how often, in American business, they keep a person just because they're afraid to fire them. We're not afraid to fire them. We don't care about being sued, because if we go to court we can show that discrimination is not our policy. But if a person is no good, he's no good, no matter whether he's black or white, or what faith he might be.

If the leadership is this way, you'd be amazed how many people will follow. We owned the Ice Capades and I said, "It's all white. Why isn't there somebody black in there?"

"Well, blacks don't skate."

"Hold a competition. Find the best black skater you can, and you work with them." We hired a black girl.

It always comes down to fairness, putting yourself in somebody else's shoes. We broke one barrier when Kennedy became president and there was a Catholic in the White House. And one of these days we'll have a Jewish president. I gave the first big money to Doug Wilder, and he became the first black governor of Virginia. One of these days we'll have a black president. [John Kluge made this prediction in 2001.]

KLUGE

Kluge Credo on Racial Equality in B'casting: "Put Up Or Shut Up"

Variety, September 11, 1963

"The time has passed for mere lip service to a policy of non-discrimination in business in general and the broadcast industry in particular. We must implement such policy in all phases of our operations." That's the credo of John H. Kluge, president of the Metromedia chain of radio-tv stations.

"As people in the communications business," Kluge said about the current Negro struggle for civil rights, "we must be in the infantry in the march of progress. We are in the most sensitive area and must show the greatest responsibility." Metromedia itself, Kluge said, does not and has not practiced any form of discrimination in its hiring policy Although no hoopla was made over this fact, Metromedia employs numerous Negroes on all levels of its operational and administrative staff, including one Negro associate director, one chief of production, and several in the legal, accounting and traffic departments.

Kluge conceded that the problem of the Negro's status in American life has not been enough in "the broadcasting conscience and consciousness." The time has come to correct this wrong, Kluge said, by positive action. "We must learn to deal with each other as human beings and not on the basis of color."

Kluge said that discriminatory practices not only hurt the Negro but the nation as a whole. "We just limit our choice of the best available people." But, he stressed, "I don't practice discrimination not because it's bad business. I wouldn't even if it were good business. Discrimination is a moral wrong and must be combated because of that."

The Metromedia exec said that the solutions will not be easy but was confident that they would be found. "In the end, better education will lead to better jobs and a more responsible role for those who have been deprived up to now. Before that stage is reached, we must expect some trouble. It's difficult for the Negroes who have been held down for so long to find a perfect balance in reaching out for their rights."

Kluge takes the long historical view of the current civil rights struggle. "Some 500 years from now, when the history of our time is written down, the people who are fighting against human equality will look like very small people indeed."

It may sound funny to you, but the reason I'm in a lot of businesses is that, basically, I don't like business. I would get very bored with one business. That isn't enough of a challenge for me.

John Kluge On Success

I'd never heard of billionaires.

In 1954, I got the phone call: "John, you're a multi-millionaire." That night I went to a movie to celebrate the event. I'd never heard of billionaires.

When *Forbes* had me listed as the richest man in America—well, I'm no longer that, far from it. And I didn't really like it. My mail increased dramatically, most of it asking for money. I respond to some of those requests but most of them... One woman sent me a letter and she said, "I need nine million dollars and not a penny more." Another woman wrote and said, "My husband's coming back from the service and I gambled away our life savings of $250,000, and if you want to save our marriage, please send me the money." I guess her marriage wasn't saved.

I don't have any empathy with people who have money whose only purpose is to make more money. Basically, I never really worked for money. I always worked for an idea, and maybe the money would follow. If it didn't follow, it didn't follow. Sure, I have a comfortable house—no mortgage and that sort of thing—but, actually, that's not where my head is. My head is to develop something which has some meaning.

My mother was really very modest. Hopefully, I learned something from her.

My mother said to me one day, "You know, the neighbors here in Detroit are telling me that they read about a John Kluge in this and that." I said to my mother, "I always get mixed up with that fellow." So she never really knew. Because no matter what I gave my mother, she would give it away. I remember I bought a new Bentley, back in the '60s, and I drove it myself. My mother and stepfather never flew, they always took a train when they came to visit. One time I picked them up in Charlottesville in the Bentley and I said to my mother, "Mom, do you like this car?" She looked around and said, "You know, this is the nicest Chevrolet I've ever been in." Any car, to my mother, was a Chevrolet. She was really very modest. Hopefully, I learned something from her.

KLUGE

Forbes magazine
Richest man in America
Making money
Chevrolet

172

February 26, 1996

$4.00 (Canada $4.50)

Forbes

The cheapskate billionaire

"I keep buying businesses that don't have earnings. The Plaza Hotel— that's not my style."
—*John Kluge*

CHAIRMAN & CHIEF EXECUTIVE OFFICER
EDITOR-IN-CHIEF

October 3, 1989

Mr. John Kluge
Albemarle House
Route 6
Box 69
Charlottesville, Virginia 22901

Dear John:

You sure knocked us all dead aboard the HIGHLANDER the other night. Me the most deadest!

First there was a wee Tiffany box and in that a stupendous Rolex which hasn't left my wrist since.

Then there was the wee pledge of one million for AmFAR which insures emmense success for both the ball and the reception which Marella Agnelli and Amalita Fortabat will join me in hosting on Friday, November 3rd in the FORBES Galleries - we're co-chairman (it takes three of us to do what Pat did last year!).

Then there was, of course, the other little gesture which made the night, the day, the week and the year for the Reagans and the Library - your second million dollar contribution.

As we joked that night at dinner, it is so expensive to be rich. But we both know many who are who don't give or give as little and tokenly as they can get away with.

John, you are a great man as well as an enormously, wonderfully, generous man. There are no adequate ways to say thank you to the degree so many feel so thankful to you.

Quite aside from your generosity, it's a ball to be your friend and the Forbeses treasure you and Pat.

Malcolm S. Forbes

eg

P.S. I knew you were a financial wizard but I didn't know your slight of hand extended to ladies' hair!

I wouldn't want my name on a bathroom door.

Believe it or not, it's more difficult to give money away in a meaningful way than it is to make it. You don't want to give it away helter skelter. You want to have a meaning. I don't want to have the gifts be an edifice for myself. The name on a building—oh, I hate that. I just hate it. There's a hospital out in California, you go in the bathroom and it's got a name on it. I wouldn't want my name on a bathroom door. But that's the way they fund it, and some people love seeing their names.

To me, it's such folly to give to causes that are secondary. I believe that if you can improve someone's mind, that will improve their children, and their children will improve their children's children. That's where the meaning comes. A building is a necessity, but that's not where I want to be. I want to be in the development of people.

The future of this country, or any country, is its young people. I chose minorities because I think quite often they're overlooked. In the Library of Congress, I have another idea, basically, and that is the Nobel Prize, a million dollars, is primarily in science. My prize of one million dollars is in the humanities—philosophy, religion. We tend to look down on the humanities—science is everything! Well, it ain't everything. So that's why I set up that prize.

KLUGE

Columbia University
Education
Philanthropy
Implementation
John W. Kluge Center at
    the Library of Congress
Humanities

I know I'm not going to own anything when I leave this world, so why not give it away before I go?

I would love to go to the grave with zero, absolutely zero. It seems to me you get more fun out of being alive and giving than when you're dead. People wonder why I give things away. I think I do that because I know I'm not going to own anything when I leave this world, so why not give it away before I go? Well, I'm always interested in implementation. As a matter of fact, I don't think an idea is worth the powder to blow it up if it isn't implemented. I think the two go hand in hand.

The chief inspiration was that I wanted to really help disadvantaged students, those who couldn't afford to go to college. I know what it was, because I was an immigrant, and an immigrant is very much disadvantaged. So Columbia gave me a scholarship, and I wanted to do the same thing for other students. I know the problems they have, because I went through it myself.

It's amazing how serious they are about achieving something and then giving back something.

It was my fiftieth reunion at Columbia and I grabbed the microphone and I said, "You know, Columbia doubled my scholarship, and as a parting gift, I'm doubling the funding I give to Columbia for this program." That's how it happened, and it just seemed appropriate.

The greatest gift I get from that is the letters I get from people who have pulled themselves up by their bootstraps, and amounted to something in the field that they chose.

What I'd like to see—and this is why the selection process is so important—is more role models in business, the professions, academics. Blacks are visible sports and music, but are they engineers? Are they doctors? Are they business people? Are they educators? Whatever they are, that they establish themselves as a role model. And it begins right there in the selection process. You're never going to be a hundred percent right, but if out of every fifty students, forty percent, twenty of them develop into role models, you know that would be a great plus.

Of what I have seen of these students the last few years, there's no question in my mind they are going to be role models. It's amazing how serious they are about achieving something and then giving back something. It's amazing how many of them are the first member of their family to go to college. When they grow up and have a family, you know if they've gone to school, their interest is to send their children to school. It starts a whole process, and the children will do the same thing with their children. And that's why I am so keen about doing something for the human mind rather than building buildings.

KLUGE

Philanthropy
Columbia University
Kluge Scholars
Education

178

Columbia College TODAY

November 2004

John Kluge '37:
Opening the Gates

Entrepreneur's generosity
enables hundreds of promising
students to attend the College
and make the most of their
campus experiences.

Cover of Columbia College's alumni magazine.
John Kluge with his wife, Tussi, flanked by three former Kluge Scholars.

Columbia to Receive $400 Million for Student Aid

From the *New York Times*, April 11, 2007

By TAMAR LEWIN

Columbia University will announce a gift of $400 million today, one of the largest ever to an American university, from John Werner Kluge, 92, a billionaire who has long been one of the university's strongest supporters.

Columbia's president, Lee Bollinger, said last night: "Obviously, this is an extraordinary gift by any standard. It's huge in its consequences and effects on the university."

The gift, which is to come from Mr. Kluge's estate when he dies, is to be used for financial aid to students, officials said. More commonly, philanthropic donations are used to pay for a new building or endow a chair.

Mr. Kluge had previously given Columbia $110 million, including his Kluge Scholars Program, which has supported more than 500 Columbia College students. It provides four-year scholarships to 40 to 60 needy students a year, chosen by the admissions office.

At Columbia's 2004 black-tie celebration of the program and his 90th birthday, Mr. Kluge discussed his commitment to scholarships.

"I'd rather by far invest in people than buildings," he said. "If I can infuse a mind to improve itself, that'll pass on to their children, and to their children's children." He also reflected on the financial aid he received at Columbia: "If it hadn't been for Columbia, my path in life would have been completely different."

Last night, Mr. Bollinger said of Mr. Kluge: "The idea of financial aid for needy students is just part of his core. He has a deep desire to improve things."

Mr. Bolinger said half of the $400 million would go to scholarships for undergraduates at Columbia College, and the other half to scholarships and fellowships in other parts of the university.

The announcement comes in the first year after Columbia announced a $4 billion fund-raising campaign emphasizing financial aid and endowed faculty across its schools and campuses.

Nearly every institution of higher learning feels an urgency to raise funds, but the pressure on Columbia is particularly acute since it competes against the wealthiest universities in the country. Last year, its endowment was more than $5 billion, one of the largest in the country but still behind other Ivy League universities.

Until now, the largest gift in the university's history was slightly more than $200 million, from the Jerome L. Greene Foundation and Mr. Greene's widow, Dawn M. Greene.

Mr. Kluge was born in Chemnitz, Germany, grew up in Detroit, and won a scholarship that allowed him to attend Columbia, where he graduated in 1937, majoring in economics.

Mr. Kluge made his fortune as a broadcasting entrepreneur, building his multimedia company, Metromedia, into the nation's largest television business before selling his television stations to Rupert Murdoch in 1986 — stations that became the core of the Fox broadcast network — and then turning his attention, increasingly, to philanthropy.

In 2000 Mr. Kluge gave $73 million to the Library of Congress for a scholarly center and other projects, including the creation of a $1 million John W. Kluge Prize for the study of humanity, intended for areas that the Nobel prizes do not cover, like political science, sociology and philosophy.

In recent years Mr. Kluge sold his 78,000-acre Scottish estate and a London townhouse and a home in Munich, and donated his Virginia farm with 35 outbuildings and thousands of acres to the University of Virginia.

Last year, Mr. Kluge was ranked 25th on the Forbes list of the 400 richest Americans, with an estimated fortune of $9.1 billion. Mr. Kluge has three children and has been divorced three times; he is now married to Maria Tussi Kluge.

According to the Chronicle of Higher Education, the largest gift to a private university was last year's $1 billion endowment from the Anil Agarwal Foundation to establish Vedanta University in India.

In the United States, the California Institute of Technology received gifts totaling $600 million in 2001 from Gordon and Betty Moore and the Gordon and Betty Moore Foundation. That same year, Stanford University received a $400 million gift from the William and Flora Hewlett Foundation. In 1997, the Franklin W. Olin College of Engineering received $460 million from the F. W. Olin Foundation.

AUSTIN QUIGLEY, former dean of Columbia College:

Kluge scholars have gone on to the best graduate schools in the country: Princeton, Yale, Harvard, Stanford, Chicago and Columbia itself. They've earned the most prestigious awards: Rhodes Scholarships, Marshall Scholarships, Fulbrights and Kelletts. They've gone on to an enormous variety of careers as lawyers, doctors, investment bankers, business entrepreneurs, musicians, actors, movie directors, government officials, researchers, etc., etc.

KIMBERLY JOHNSON, professor at Barnard:

It is now that I think I feel the full impact that the Kluge Program has made to me. As a professor who is a woman of color, I have had an impact on the lives of dozens of young women at Barnard and Columbia. For them I reflect a new possibility that academia can be and should be a place where the life of the mind is open to all. I've also become a mentor to young women, pushing them, whether they want it or not, to expand their horizons and live up to the wonderful potential that all of us have. As a scholar and as a teacher and as a mentor, I believe that the Kluge Program has not only benefited me directly, but also my students, my colleagues, and my profession.

MIGNON MOORE, professor at Columbia:

There are so many bright and talented minority youth who simply do not have the financial resources and social networks to help them attend and complete four years of high quality undergraduate education at a prestigious school like Columbia. Your program will ensure that more of these deserving students continue to have that opportunity. Thank you for choosing Columbia for your philanthropic generosity, and thank you for encouraging and supporting minority students from historically underrepresented groups. Your presence in our undergraduate lives was indirect yet critical to our success. Please know that your work at Columbia has not only helped to provide individual students with a quality education, but has also helped to ensure the continued upward social and economic mobility of a generation of young women and men.

And what more can you ask, really?

Power never did interest me, and the reason for it is I am much more in tune with people doing what they want to do, not what I want them to do. The need for power, I don't know where it comes from, but it was never one of my needs. I'm perfectly willing and able to live out a life of not being known. I'd like to disappear.

I'm pleased by these students' successes and proud of my role—but the most important thing is the student. You can create the opportunity but if the student doesn't take advantage of it, it's meaningless.

You know, the world is divided between thinkers and doers, and after meeting the scholars, I felt a lot of these people were both. A lot of them have come from homes where they are the first ones to have an education, and they take their responsibility seriously. They think about their careers, they think about their role in life much more than your average student. They appreciate anything that's done for them, and I am sure in many years to come some of them will not only bring a lot of great honor to the institution, but they will help the institution financially.

And what more could you ask, really?

THE RAIN MAKER

A few years ago, *The New York Times* quoted one of the bankers saying that I'm the only ninety-year-old that has a thirty-year time vision. I don't mean to imply that I'm going to live forever, because I'm not, but why limit the dream to what you think your life expectancy is?

John Kluge On Life Expectancy

Photo Credits

Unless otherwise noted, all images and photographs are drawn from the papers of John W. Kluge, held by the Kluge Center at the Library of Congress.